W9-BMY-845

DATE DUE

Demco, Inc. 38-293

For Clara Margaret McCluskey, who never ceases to inspire me.

Writing for Understanding

Strategies to Increase Content Learning

Understanding

Donovan R. Walling

CORWIN

A SAGE Company

313654554

11-30-09

For information:

Corwin
A SAGE Company
2455 Teller Road
Thousand Oaks, California 91320
(800) 233-9936
Fax: (800) 417-2466
www.corwinpress.com

SAGE Ltd.
1 Oliver's Yard
55 City Road
London EC1Y 1SP
United Kingdom

SAGE Pvt. Ltd.
B 1/I 1 Mohan Cooperative
   Industrial Area
Mathura Road,
New Delhi 110 044
India

SAGE Asia-Pacific Pte. Ltd.
33 Pekin Street #02-01
Far East Square
Singapore 048763

Printed in the United States of America

Library of Congress Cataloging-in-Publication Data

Walling, Donovan R., 1948-
Writing for understanding: strategies to increase content learning / Donovan R. Walling.
      p. cm.
Includes bibliographical references and index.
ISBN 978-1-4129-6434-0 (cloth)
ISBN 978-1-4129-6435-7 (pbk.)
   1. English language—Composition and exercises—Study and teaching (Secondary)
2. Language arts—Correlation with content subjects. I. Title.

LB1631.W233 2009
372.62'3044—dc22   2009020546

This book is printed on acid-free paper.

09   10   11   12   13   10   9   8   7   6   5   4   3   2   1

Acquisitions Editor:	Cathy Hernandez
Editorial Assistant:	Sarah Bartlett
Production Editor:	Veronica Stapleton
Copy Editor:	Tomara Kafka
Typesetter:	C&M Digitals (P) Ltd.
Proofreader:	Dennis W. Webb
Indexer:	Molly Hall
Cover Designer:	Karine Hovsepian

Contents

Acknowledgments

The author wishes to acknowledge the support of colleagues in the Sheboygan (Wisconsin) Area School District; the Department of Defense Dependents Schools; the Carmel-Clay Schools of Carmel, Indiana; the Monroe County Community School District in Bloomington, Indiana; Ivy Tech in Bloomington; the University of Wisconsin-Milwaukee; Indiana University, and the Bloomington Playwrights Project. The wisdom and guidance over many years by friends, colleagues, and mentors too numerous to name have contributed to this book.

Corwin gratefully acknowledges the contributions of the following reviewers:

Sherry L. Annee
Science Department Chairperson and Biotechnology Instructor
Brebeuf Jesuit Preparatory School
Indianapolis, IN

William E. Doll Jr.
Emeritus Professor of Curriculum and Instruction
Louisiana State University University of Victoria
Baton Rouge, LA

and

Adjunct Professor
University of Victoria
Victoria, BC, Canada

Linda Fitzharris
Associate Professor
Department of Elementary,
   Early Childhood, and Middle Grades Education
College of Charleston
Charleston, SC

Hector Ibarra
Sixth and Seventh Grade Teacher
Science Department Chair
West Branch Middle School
West Branch, IA

Sharon Kane
Professor of Curriculum and Instruction
State University of New York at Oswego
Warners, NY

Judith Lapointe
Pearland, TX

Bob Loyd
Associate Professor
Department of Special Education
Armstrong Atlantic State University
Savannah, GA

Lyneille Meza
Coordinator of Data and Assessment
Denton ISD
Denton, TX

Rose Reissman
President
New York City Association of Teachers of English
New York, NY

Deb Teitelbaum
Graduate Research Assistant
Department of Educational Administration and Policy
University of Georgia
Athens, GA

Ruth Thomas
Professor and Department Chair
Curriculum and Instruction Department
College of Education and Human Development
University of Minnesota
Minneapolis, MN

About the Author

Donovan R. Walling is a writer, editor, educator, and consultant. He serves as a senior consultant for the Center for Civic Education. He has taught art, English, and journalism in the United States and abroad and has worked as a curriculum administrator in public school districts in Wisconsin and Indiana. From 1993 until 2006, he was director of publications for the education association Phi Delta Kappa International.

Walling is the author or editor of more than a dozen professional books for educators and numerous articles and other publications. He is nationally recognized in the field of art education, where some of his publications include *Under Construction: The Role of the Arts and Humanities in Postmodern Schooling* (Phi Delta Kappa Educational Foundation, 1997); the Corwin books *Rethinking How Art Is Taught: A Critical Convergence* (2000) and *Visual Knowing: Connecting Art and Ideas Across the Curriculum* (2005); the core chapter on visual and performing arts for the Association for Supervision and Curriculum Development's *Curriculum Handbook* (2002); and the "Art in the Schools" entry for Macmillan's *Encyclopedia of Education* (2003).

Walling's recent books include *Public Education, Democracy, and the Common Good* (Phi Delta Kappa Educational Foundation, 2004) and *Teaching Writing to Visual, Auditory, and Kinesthetic Learners* (Corwin, 2006).

The author can be reached at drwalling@gmail.com.

Introduction

How Can I Teach Writing if I'm Not a Writing Teacher?

First things first: This book is *not* about teaching writing. It's about *using* writing as an instructional tool for increasing students' understanding of content. Therefore, it is written for non-language arts teachers with approaches and strategies that are applicable from the upper elementary grades through high school.

Writing increases understanding in all content areas, whether math or science, social studies or foreign language, art or music, or physical education. And you don't need to be a writing teacher in order to use writing as an instructional tool any more than you need to be a computer programmer to use a computer or an auto mechanic to drive a car.

The goal of this book is to show readers—teachers and prospective teachers—how to use writing as an integral part of effective instruction, not to turn you into writing teachers. There are many reasons why writing increases students' understanding of content and many easy-to-use but highly effective strategies that teachers can integrate into existing lessons in order to heighten student achievement. Both the reasons and the strategies will be explored in the chapters that follow, but here's a sample of what to expect.

As a content specialist, who better than you to get students writing about the ideas and concepts that drive understanding of your content area? You know—as do effective teachers everywhere—that asking students simply to acquire knowledge through listening or reading does not lead to full understanding. The goal of effective instruction is more than acquisition of information. We want our students to be able to use the information they gain, to apply it in both familiar and unfamiliar contexts, to manipulate it, to distill it, to roll in it mentally until it becomes part of the fabric of their minds. Until this higher level of understanding is reached, students cannot truly use content knowledge. They may be able to regurgitate facts for a short-answer test—and forget them soon afterward—but they often cannot use new information in other contexts or connect new content understandings to existing knowledge.

Why does writing make a difference? An old Chinese proverb says:

I hear . . . and I forget.

I see . . . and I remember.

I do . . . and I understand.

Writing is part of "doing." It activates learning. Let's take an example from a science class and examine how students might increase their understanding of a lesson through writing. An introductory lesson about oxygen and combustion might proceed this way:

First, the teacher tells students that oxygen is necessary for burning. (*I hear and I forget.*)

Next, the teacher says, "Let me show you an example," and stands a lighted tea candle on a rubber mat. Then the teacher places an upturned glass or clear jar over the candle. Students watch as the candle flame goes out. (*I see and I remember.*) Finally, the teacher asks the students to pair off with their own candles and jars, saying, "Try it yourselves." (*I do and I understand.*)

At this point, the teacher has accomplished a basic goal. Students know that a candle flame will go out if the lighted candle is placed into a glass jar so that air cannot get inside to replenish the oxygen used by the flame. But no good teacher, even at the most elementary level, would stop at this point. The next logical question is to ask students, "When you put a lighted candle in a closed jar, *why* does the flame go out?" Depending on the age of the students, they may put forward various theories or simply state the obvious: the burning flame uses up enough oxygen so that too little remains to sustain the fire, and so the candle goes out. (Advanced classes also will be able to explore other facets of this and similar experiments, such as the production of water vapor, the role of carbon dioxide, and so forth. But the oxygen-combustion connection is sufficient for this example.)

In some cases, this is where the lesson ends. That's unfortunate because this fundamental knowledge has broad applicability if students are allowed and encouraged to make the knowledge truly their own through deeper understanding. The students will remember that oxygen is necessary for the candle to keep burning, but will they be able to take that principle of combustion and apply it to other contexts?

This is the teachable moment at which using writing as an instructional tool can help deepen and expand students' understanding. For example, the teacher might ask students to write in their science journals, prompted by one or more of the following questions:

- You are standing close to a campfire to stay warm when suddenly your pant leg catches fire. You remember the safety lesson about "stop, drop, and roll." So you quickly drop to the ground and roll until the fire goes out. Explain why this safety technique works.
- The local newspaper carries a story about a car fire. Firefighters used foam to put out the blaze. Describe the science behind this firefighting technique. Speculate on why using hoses and water might not be as effective for putting out a car fire.
- You are frying a hamburger in a skillet when all at once the grease in the pan catches fire. You remember being told never to throw water on a grease fire because it can spread the fire and make matters worse. So you calmly reach over and put a lid on the skillet, and the flames go out. How is this technique for controlling a fire on your stove like the candle-flame experiment?
- Think about astronauts in space. Space often is characterized as "airless," meaning that there is little or no oxygen in space. After all, isn't that why astronauts wear spacesuits? If space is airless, suppose that a part on a space station needed to be repaired by welding it while the station is orbiting the earth. How might that be accomplished? Once you have written down your ideas, research this topic and see if you can confirm your answer.

Writing for understanding often can be thought of as writing to reflect on ideas. Southern author Eudora Welty (1984) once commented, "In writing, as in life, the connections of all sorts of relationships and kinds lie in wait of discovery, and give out their signals to the Geiger counter of the charged imagination, once it is drawn into the right field" (p. 99). As students write in their journals in response to one of the preceding prompts, they are reflecting on the experiment that they witnessed and replicated. They are being asked to consider: What does this experiment really show me? How is this experiment related to the situation in the question? What is the *big idea*—that is, the general principle—and how can this idea be applied in other situations?

Students' answers are food for further discussion, clarification, and extension. Reflective writing, such as science journal responses, are not "public" in the sense that they are not intended to be read, much less graded, by the teacher. Reflective writing provides a way for students to think *intentionally*. It's easy to say to students, "Now think about this experiment and how you might apply this principle to some other situation." But in many cases, not much critical thinking will go on, certainly not much organized thinking. Asking students to write is a way of helping students reflect on ideas in an intentional, organized way. Teachers do not need to read this type of writing. Indeed, it's probably better if they don't. (Later chapters will explain why.)

But, you might ask, "If I don't read students' journals, will they take the writing seriously?" The short answer is yes—if you establish the importance of writing for understanding as part of the ethos of your class-room. One way to do so is to *use* students' writing in various ways. For example, ask a few students to volunteer to read their reflections to the class in order to propel discussion. This is a way not only of extending the reflection and stimulating further thought but also of validating students' writing efforts.

"Don't I have to grade students' writing?" The short answer is no. Following are five alternatives to "grading" students' writing.

Monitor students' writing behaviors by allowing class time specifically for reflective writing. This is a management-by-walking-around strategy. Move around the classroom to observe students in the act of writing. Stop and ask a question if a student seems puzzled or hesitant.

Register students' writing activity. Acknowledge students' efforts as you move about the classroom. Check off that students have done the writing assignment. This doesn't require reading or grading the written work. It merely notes that students have made the effort and been recognized for it.

Discuss students' ideas. Encourage students to read aloud what they have written as a way to initiate and propel class discussion. Having written reflectively, students now have something to say. They aren't being called on for a spur-of-the-moment response. Writing provides starting points, and the reflection already evident in the writing allows the discussion to proceed at a high level.

Critique students' conclusions, for example, by pairing students to share their writing with one another. Ask students to find key ideas in their peers' work and to ask questions for clarification. When students read their writing aloud to the whole class, be prepared to do the same. Point out how students have been insightful and ask questions to draw out additional ideas.

Correct students' misunderstandings. When students share their written reflections, it is easy to identify content misunderstandings and faulty interpretations and to correct them. Correction at this point can save future reteaching.

All of these strategies, which will be explored in greater depth, engage students in *using* writing to develop and deepen understanding of content. None requires the teacher to read or grade the writing. Indeed, Glasgow and Farrell (2007) believe,

> Experienced teachers recognize that writing skill develops on a continuum, and they help their students to see individual growth along that continuum. Students who understand that what they have to say is unique and valuable are much more likely to risk committing their thoughts and ideas to paper. They know that the mechanical components of writing can be addressed concretely father along in their writing process. (p. 91)

The chapters that follow show how to use writing as a tool for increasing students' understanding of content. Chapter 1 provides an overview of how writing increases understanding and why using writing as strategic instruction is important in order to meet challenging curricular standards and the requirements of high-stakes testing. Chapters 2 through 6 describe how to develop specific types of writing assignments. These types, or genres, include narrative, descriptive, expository, argumentative, and persuasive writing. All of these types are valuable in every content area, as examples will demonstrate.

Chapter 7 draws together the preceding chapters to examine how writing can be used in ways that engage students in discussions—termed classroom and student dialogues—that both validate students' understandings and enhance them. Chapter 8 focuses on connections between writing and the Internet and includes a number of online resources for teachers and students. Online writing opportunities can stimulate student writing, and online resources can help students and teachers get the most out of their writing endeavors. Chapter 9 offers a troubleshooting guide in the form of FAQs (frequently asked questions) about writing, in particular about standard writing conventions. The straightforward answers make it easier to use writing as an effective teaching tool for increasing students' content knowledge and understanding. Finally, Chapter 10 provides an annotated compilation of books and downloadable online resources that teachers may find useful in further exploring how to use writing for strategic teaching and learning.

A note about student writing examples: Most are composites for the sake of illustration. In almost all cases, any usage and spelling errors have been corrected to maintain the focus on content. None of the student names refer to real persons.

The idea behind writing for understanding has a long history. The phrase "writing for understanding"—sometimes rendered as "writing to learn"—is used or implied in countless books and other resources for curriculum and instruction, many of which are referenced in various chapters. An excellent example at the collegiate level is the Writing-in-the-Major Project at the University of Wisconsin-La Crosse that, according to its Website, "establishes department-based programs to advance students' capacities in formal writing and writing-to-learn" (www.uwlax.edu/wimp/index.htm, accessed January 3, 2008). Much of what visitors find at this Website can be adapted for pre-collegiate classrooms.

The notion of writing for understanding rests on constructivist learning theory—that is, students construct their own understanding based on integrating new information with existing knowledge. Students are not empty vessels into which information is poured. Rather they are repositories of experiences wherein new ideas are connected with already acquired information to construct new understanding. Writing is a vehicle for increasing and strengthening such connections.

1

How Writing Increases Understanding

We remember Ernest Hemingway for his rugged fiction. But in 1932 he published a nonfiction book titled *Death in the Afternoon,* an analysis of Spanish bullfighting that examines fear and courage. In describing the ceremony and traditions of bullfighting, Hemingway also famously said of writing: "Prose is architecture, not interior decoration" (Hemingway, 1932, p. 191). Readers of Hemingway will recognize this philosophy realized in the terse, controlled prose of his familiar novels, such as *The Sun Also Rises* and *A Farewell to Arms.*

In this book, *Writing for Understanding,* the central theme echoes Hemingway's dictum: prose is the architecture of understanding. Each time students write, they are building, literally, brick by brick, word by word, increased understanding of subject matter. This does not mean, however, that each piece of student writing will or must be a polished gem. Most pieces, in fact, will simply be rough bricks. The strategies in this book are not specifically intended to help teachers turn students into accomplished writers, though practice in writing invariably is time well spent. Rather, the strategies are designed to help teachers incorporate meaningful student writing assignments into daily instruction to increase students' understanding of content.

Prose

Written or spoken language in ordinary form—that is, without metrical structure. Poetry, which usually has a metrical structure, often is viewed as the counterpoint to prose.

Does this mean that writing conventions—correct spelling, grammar, punctuation—should be ignored? Of course not. It is simply a matter of focus, and the focus for teachers who are not writing teachers per se is content: mathematics, science, history, civics, art, drama, music, physical education, health, and so on. For example, mathematics teachers can increase students' understanding of content by using writing assignments to elicit explanations of how students have solved various problems. At the same time, most students *will* improve their writing skills simply through practice and peer interaction about writing, without direct instruction in writing conventions. (For the sake of convenience, however, readers will find that Chapter 9 addresses a number of the most frequently asked questions about writing conventions.)

Think of this first chapter as a course, Architecture of Writing 101. My purpose is to explore how writing increases students' understanding of content—regardless of subject matter or students' abilities—and to dispel common myths and misconceptions that get in the way of using writing as an effective instructional tool.

DEBUNKING MYTHS AND MISCONCEPTIONS

Many teachers, unless they are directly responsible for teaching writing, shy away from having students write substantive text. There seems to be a general fear—even among some language arts teachers—that asking students to write more than a few words will inevitably lead to more work for both students and teachers with minimal gain in learning. Many teachers believe that assigning writing is a "Catch-22" situation. Parents, teacher supervisors, and students will *expect* every writing assignment to be corrected, which teachers don't have time to do, nor do many teachers feel competent or comfortable doing so. This leads teachers to question whether having students write really improves students' writing *or* learning.

It's best to dispense with a few myths and misconceptions related to these concerns at the start. Let's begin with the first concern.

Myth 1: All writing must be corrected.

This is a common misconception that should be dispelled on the first day of class. Writing for understanding means that students will write many types of prose for a variety of purposes. Virtually none of this writing will need to be read by the teacher with an eye to correcting grammar and punctuation, which is what most parents, teacher supervisors, and students mean when they talk about *correcting*—in other words, marking or red-penciling—students' written work. In some cases, such as writing to reflect on new information, students' writing will not be intended for the teacher to read at all. In self-reflective writing, such as journaling, the student writer is his or her own intended reader. In other instances, students may share their writing with peers, with or without teacher intervention.

When introducing writing for understanding as an instructional strategy, it will be helpful to explain this approach in advance: to the teacher supervisor to gain support; to students so that they understand how writing will be used in their studies; and to parents, by a newsletter sent home or during an early open house, so that they understand your approach as well.

Myth 2: All writing must be graded.

This misconception pairs with the preceding one. It may be helpful to incorporate a check-off system to encourage students to keep up with writing tasks, but assigning a grade to most of the writing assignments described in this book is unnecessary and can be counterproductive. Grades are value markers. Students may get mistaken impressions of the value of some tasks over others. This assignment is graded; therefore, it is important. This assignment is not graded; therefore, it's not important. In fact, non-graded writing assignments may be more valuable in increasing content understandings than fully developed or graded writing.

Writing done to increase understanding of content is important not in the particulars—this answer or that journal entry—but in the aggregate. In other words, the process of thinking and composing is more important as an instructional strategy than the product, the written text. As with the correcting of students' writing, it will be beneficial to explain in advance to students and others how written work will be graded and, more important, why much of students' writing will not be graded.

Myth 3: Students' writing won't improve without teacher feedback.

Certainly some writing problems will not get corrected without direct instruction. However, in many cases, students *do* correct their own writing as they develop self-awareness as writers. They read other students' prose. They comment on one another's writing. With time and practice, most students improve their ability to express ideas cogently in writing.

Writing is like any skill. Whether a student is learning to serve a tennis ball, to solve a complex equation, or to draw a convincing looking apple, practice improves performance. The same is true for writing. Feedback from teachers and peers helps, of course. But real improvement in writing comes, as it does in all skill development, when the student takes charge of learning by building self-awareness that leads to self-correction and increased understanding.

Myth 4: Written responses to questions are no more effective than short answers (true–false, multiple choice, fill in the blank) for increasing student learning.

On the contrary, prose responses require more complete, usually more complex thinking than short answers. True-false, multiple-choice, and other types of short-answer questions rarely can be structured to require or encourage higher level thinking. To take a cue from Bloom's familiar taxonomy of cognition (Bloom & Krathwohl, 1956), most short-answer questions ask students to think at the lowest levels: demonstrating knowledge or comprehension (remembering or understanding) by repeating or reproducing information. In contrast, well-constructed questions that require prose responses can push students toward higher level thinking: applying, analyzing, synthesizing, and evaluating information. Bloom's taxonomy is illustrated in Figure 1.1.

Figure 1.1   Bloom's Taxonomy

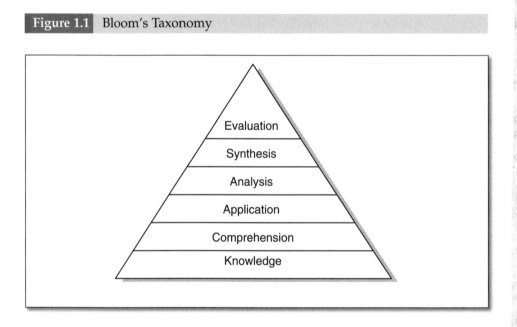

Following is a typical true-false question:

Seventy-five percent is the same as three-fourths. True or false?

The student must recall this specific fact or be able to make the mathematical conversion in order to choose *true* as the correct response. At most, this item requires simple application. But it is also possible that the student just remembered this particular equivalence without being able to make the computation. There is no way for the teacher to judge the depth of a student's learning from this type of question. It would take several questions of the same character to do that.

On the other hand, a prose-response item might be stated as follows:

Explain how to convert three-fourths to a percentage.

Alternatives to Bloom

Since the mid-1950s when Bloom's cognitive domain taxonomy was published (along with affective and psychomotor taxonomies), a number of writers and theorists have tinkered with this familiar classification system without, in my view, improving it much. Mary Forehand (2005) provides a succinct overview of recent developments.

In this case, students must first recall the pertinent information, then apply it, and finally describe the process. Writing the explanation requires remembering, understanding, applying, and analyzing—in other words, the same cognitive starting points as the true-false question *plus* higher level thinking in terms of analysis and description. From the students' responses to this type of question, the teacher can readily discern how well students understand the concept and decide whether to reteach or move on to other content.

Myth 5: Getting students to write will take more time than it's worth.

When teachers commit to making writing an integral part of teaching and learning, writing activities simply become part of the natural instructional flow for both teachers and students. It does take higher level thinking on the part of teachers as well as students. At first, this may seem to be more time-consuming, but with practice, most teachers will find that prose-response questions require no more time to develop than short-answer questions—and usually they will need fewer prose responses to assess students' mastery of content.

Effective writing assignments will certainly demand more higher level thinking of students. And, yes, thinking deeply about content and writing prose responses do take more time than rote or superficial thinking and true-false, fill-in-the-blank, and multiple-choice responding. But—and this is an important *but*—the payoff is greater depth of understanding. The ripple effects of deeper content knowledge include:

- Students tackle advanced subject matter more readily and more successfully than they would on a base of superficial knowledge.
- Students perform better on assessments of content knowledge, especially those high-stakes tests that depend on a broad knowledge base rather than an understanding of specific course content.

There is general consensus in the education community that middle and high school students do not write as much or as well as they should in order to meet the communication demands that they will face in further education and the world of work. The 2007 National Assessment of Educational Progress (NAEP) writing assessment found that more eighth- and twelfth-grade students now master "basic" writing than was the case in previous assessments, in 1998 and 2002. However, only a much smaller percentage—33 percent of eighth-graders and 24 percent of twelfth-graders—are *proficient* writers (Salahu-Din, Persky, & Miller, 2008). Proficient refers to the skills needed to write a successful school essay or to explain complex information.

FIVE RESEARCH-BASED *TRUTHS* ABOUT WRITING

It seems fair to trade five myths for five truths. One overarching truth is that writing is underused as an instructional strategy. Following are, in brief, five more specific truths about writing that teachers should consider as they plan for optimal instruction. Like most truths in life, these are not new. The first four, in fact, come from research done by Judith A. Langer and Arthur N. Applebee (1987) twenty years ago. Some truths simply don't go out of date.

Truth 1: Writing involves conscious manipulation of content, which improves understanding.

"In general," Langer and Applebee (1987) comment, "any kind of written response leads to better performance than does reading without writing" (p. 130). Why? The answer lies in the manipulation of content. As students write, they must recall information, apply it in new contexts, describe it, explain it, analyze it, summarize it, criticize it, and so forth. They use the whole range of thinking, from lower level recall to higher level evaluation, as they shape their written responses. The more students write, the more they manipulate content. Thus the more they remember and understand.

According to Langer and Applebee's (1987) analysis,

> within groups of students who complete the same tasks, students who write at greater length tend to perform better than students who write less, even after allowing for a general tendency for better students to do better at everything. (p. 130)

Truth 2: Writing improves understanding of content that is the specific focus of the writing.

The studies included in Langer and Applebee's (1987) analysis suggest that the positive learning effects of writing are *highly specific*. Students learn most about the content that they examine in their writing. Just because students examine in depth a particular idea or section of text does not mean that they will examine the entire text with the same degree of care. This understanding points to two instructional cues. Langer and Applebee (1987) state the first of these directly, "that the particular writing task chosen may matter a great deal, depending upon a teacher's objectives" (p. 131). Implicitly, this understanding also should prompt teachers to ask students to write often to increase the amount of content that is given in-depth attention.

Writing also can be a means of implementing formative assessment—that is, using writing to check for understanding. Fisher and Frey (2007) point out, "During content-area instruction, student writing can be used to determine what students know, what they still need to know, and what they are confused about" (p. 61). They also quote Kuhrt and Farris (1990), who believe, "The upper reaches of Bloom's taxonomy could not be reached without the use of some form of writing" (p. 437). Popham (2008) suggests that "instruction, if properly conceptualized and skillfully implemented, can be effective without any formative assessment whatsoever" (p. 51). But, they continue:

> *It is less likely to be,* and here's why. The function of formative assessment is to help teachers and students decide whether they need to make any adjustments in what they're doing. . . . Many teachers' instructional procedures and many students' learning tactics need major or minor adjustments. . . . In short, formative assessment serves as a sensible monitoring strategy for both teachers and students. (p. 51) (emphasis in original)

Students' written assignments thus may also serve to monitor not only general content understanding but, as Langer and Applebee (1987) suggest, understanding of specific content.

Truth 3: Writing that broadly considers content increases general understanding, while writing that is more narrowly focused increases depth of understanding.

Writing tasks such as taking notes, answering comprehension questions, and summarizing tend to "focus attention across a text as a whole" and therefore "lead to relatively superficial manipulation of the material being reviewed" (Applebee & Langer, 1987, p. 131). However, when a student engages in analytic writing tasks concentrated on more specific information, then the writer's attention also is "more directly focused on the relationships that give structure and coherence to that information" (Applebee & Langer, 1987, p. 131). Considering these relationships will inform teachers' choices of writing tasks. For example, for some content, it will be more effective to focus narrowly on certain concepts and relationships among them if understanding such relationships is more important than remembering a large body of facts.

Mansilla and Gardner (2008) contend that for students to thrive not only in school learning but in lifelong learning, they "must develop the capacity to think like experts" (p. 19). This concept gets at the notion of content selection. To nurture what Gardner, in particular, has termed the "disciplined mind" (see Gardner, 1999), teachers need to (1) help students identify essential topics in the discipline, (2) ask or allow students to spend considerable time on these few topics and study them deeply, (3) help students approach the topics in various ways, and (4) in so doing, help students develop performance understandings—that is, be able to "think with knowledge in multiple novel situations" (Mansilla & Gardner, 2008, p. 19).

Truth 4: Writing that considers unfamiliar ideas increases student understanding, whereas writing about content that is familiar may do little to increase understanding.

Langer and Applebee (1987) draw this commonsense conclusion, which sounds like merely a truism. But how often is assigned writing redundant in just this way? If students are asked to write about content they already know well, what more are they expected to learn? Theoretically, of course, one can always find keener nuances in any subject matter. But that is no longer writing for understanding as it is meant in this book.

Furthermore, writing for the purpose of increasing students' understanding of content should not be confused with having students write to demonstrate an understanding they already possess. This is not to say that writing as demonstration has no place. After all, that is the type of writing commonly found on essay tests. And to an extent that also is the nature of writing as formative assessment. But writing for understanding is not intended to test students' knowledge per se. Of course it may inform teachers about students' prior knowledge or level of concept mastery as an integral part of increasing students' understanding. In the main, the strategies in this book are aimed specifically at increasing students' knowledge and understanding of content.

Truth 5: Writing supports learning for students at various levels of English proficiency.

In recent decades, schools have seen increasing linguistic diversity coupled with the development of new ways to address the learning needs of students who are nonnative speakers of English. Writing for understanding is a particularly powerful tool for increasing content mastery by English language learners (ELLs). A recently published eight-year study by Carol Booth Olson and Robert Land (2007) found that ELLs benefited from the cognitive strategies approach to reading and writing about challenging texts, and especially demonstrated significant progress from analyzing and revising their own essays. (p. 296)

Olson and Land (2007) refer to an article by Langer and Applebee (1986), which preceded the volume cited in Truths 1–4, to define "cognitive strategies approach" as

> to make visible for students what it is that experienced readers and writers do when they compose; to introduce the cognitive strategies that underlie reading and writing in meaningful contexts; and to provide enough sustained, guided practice that students can internalize these strategies and perform complex tasks independently. (p. 274)

The writing for understanding strategies suggested in this book are specifically designed to implement a cognitive approach in which students write in meaningful contexts often so that, over time and through practice, they gain content knowledge and deepen understanding.

DEVELOPING EFFECTIVE WRITING QUESTIONS AND PROMPTS

In order for students to expand and enhance content understanding through writing, they must use higher level thinking. This means that teachers must structure writing questions and prompts that elicit such thinking. Kenneth R. Chuska (2003) makes the case this way:

> The content of a teacher's questions will determine what students perceive as important. Low-level questions call for only factual information, and if these are the only questions that are asked, students will believe that correct, right, single answers are most important. However, questions that prompt students to use their knowledge, experiences, backgrounds, beliefs, and intuition will give student a broader perspective and a sense of importance from contributing original ideas. (p. 12)

One way to think about how to develop effective questions, or writing prompts that function similarly, is to consider what journalists call the five W's and one H: who, what, when, where, why, and how. These are the questions that should be answered in the lead of a news story. They also are good starting points for classroom writing assignments—but with a caveat or two.

Teachers should bear in mind what kinds of responses these question words will elicit. *Who* can be answered with a name, *what* with one or two words of description, *when* with a date or a time, and *where* with a place.

These questions don't usually evoke much real writing. *Why* and *how,* on the other hand, require students to respond by reasoning and explaining. In many cases, it is important for students to know those who's, what's, when's, and where's. But those are starting points, not ends in themselves. An easy way to expand a basic *who-what-when-where* question is to add a secondary question that asks for the explanation. Here's an example of a straightforward *who* question:

Who painted the mural *Guernica?*

Answer: Pablo Picasso.

If students are studying art history, for example, this is a perfectly reasonable question. But it focuses on simple identification, and no real writing is needed. By the way, having students answer in a complete sentence ("Pablo Picasso painted *Guernica.*") doesn't make this a writing question. A question that elicits a written response should ask students to look deeper into the subject matter. A secondary question can be used to move students beyond identification into writing for deeper understanding. For example,

---

Who painted the mural *Guernica?* Why did the artist paint this mural?

Answer: Pablo Picasso painted *Guernica* as a protest against the German bombing of the small Spanish town of Guernica during the Spanish Civil War. He wanted the world to witness the injustice of this action through his painting.

Now the teacher and the student have opened a door to further learning and discussion. From this particular question and answer, a lesson might delve into topics as wide-ranging as artistic symbolism, the value of protest art in the past and today, or the history of the Spanish Civil War and the social and political conditions leading to World War II.

Writing questions can also take the form of writing prompts, which are statements. For example, the above question could be stated as follows:

Identify the artist who painted *Guernica* and explain the artist's reasons for making this image.

Writing prompts can be used to direct students' written responses toward more specific forms, in this case, identification and explanation. Figure 1.2 lists additional questions or prompt terms that can be used to activate higher level thinking.

Figure 1.2	Higher Level Thinking Activators

How and *why* are questions that tend to activate higher level thinking and responding. Following are some other higher level thinking activators:

Analyze	Devise	Outline
Argue	Discuss	Plan
Assess	Distinguish	Predict
Categorize	Examine	Prioritize
Classify	Explain	Propose
Compare	Formulate	Rate
Compose	Illustrate	Recommend
Construct	Imagine	Restate
Contrast	Interpret	Show
Create	Invent	Solve
Debate	Investigate	Translate
Describe	Judge	Use
Design	Justify	Verify

The focus of a lesson and the grade level of the students will determine the extent to which questions or prompts like these are used and the sophistication of response that can be expected. The sample question and prompt above are as effective for sixth-graders as for high school seniors. The nature and depth of the responses will vary. Teachers will be able to build subsequent discussions and future writing questions and prompts to match students' levels of content knowledge and understanding. Following is an example to illustrate this point.

What was Paul Revere's ride, and why is it famous?

Upper elementary or middle school student's response: Paul Revere rode through the towns to warn people that the British were coming. The British army wanted to arrest some important American leaders to make the Americans stop rebelling against the king. Paul Revere's ride is famous because Henry Wadsworth Longfellow wrote a poem about it.

High school student's response: Paul Revere was asked to ride from Boston to Lexington to warn John Hancock and Samuel Adams that the British army was on the march. The army planned to arrest them. In small towns along the way, Revere warned other patriots about the British army's movements. Revere's ride probably would have been lost to history except that Henry Wadsworth Longfellow wrote a poem about it. Longfellow's "Paul Revere's Ride" was written nearly one hundred years after the famous event, but it was published widely. The poem made the ride into a kind of myth. Today everyone knows about the midnight ride of Paul Revere because of this poem.

The development of effective writing questions and prompts will be further explored in the chapters that follow. Each of the next five chapters concentrates on eliciting a different mode (type or genre) of writing from students: narrative, descriptive, expository, argumentative, and persuasive. Some of these descriptors may seem unfamiliar—they will be to most students at first—and so each of these chapters begins with a clear definition and proceeds from there.

DAILY WRITING

Writing for understanding is most effective when students write often. Daily writing fills this need in a certain way, and once a pattern of writing is established it is easy to maintain and build upon. Daily writing, in the sense intended here, may or may not be connected to a larger project in any significant way. It may be a lesson starter or a discussion starter or a way of encouraging students to settle themselves mentally and physically to begin learning.

One strategy for daily writing is to begin each class period with a writing question posted somewhere in the classroom. Most teachers find it fairly easy to establish a consistent routine so that students come into the classroom and immediately set to work independently writing a response to this question while the teacher goes about the usual business of taking attendance and such. But this should be more than merely a settling-in exercise that is quickly abandoned. Instead, this writing moment can be used for

- Reviewing a previous lesson before continuing on the same topic
- Activating prior knowledge before starting a new lesson
- Arousing interest or curiosity about content to be studied

The writing that students do in response to the daily question is intended to be brief—just enough to get the mental juices flowing, so to speak—and to set the stage for the rest of the class period.

Here's how to use this strategy:

1. Write a question or a prompt that requires higher level thinking but can be answered in four or five sentences. (See the samples in Figure 1.3.)

2. Write, post, or project the question so that students see it the moment they come into the classroom.

3. Establish a pattern of behavior so that students enter the classroom and immediately begin to write. Ask students to use a separate journal or a separate section of their notebook. Then allow about five minutes for writing. Once this pattern is set, students will follow it without teacher direction.

4. Ask a few students to read what they have written. Use these responses to move into discussion, direct instruction, or some other aspect of the day's lesson.

Figure 1.3 Sample Daily Writing Questions and Prompts

Review a Previous Lesson

- Explain how you know that a number is a prime number.
- In your own words, define *ecosystem.*
- What did protesters hope to gain by dumping a shipment of tea into Boston Harbor?

Activate Prior Knowledge

- Have you heard the term *variable*? Describe what you think it means.
- In what ways do you think organisms resemble one another within a species?
- Briefly describe how you think that cell activity in the body might be regulated.

Arouse Interest or Curiosity

- You want to carpet your bedroom. How might you decide how much carpet to buy?
- If you were to devise a train to run by magnetic energy, what properties of magnets would you need to consider?
- It's the late 1700s, and an enemy army has landed on shore near your town. Speculate on ways that you might warn people in other nearby towns without modern means of communication.

This last step is critical. By being asked to share what they have written, students are taught (1) that writing is part of learning, (2) that such writing assignments are integral to the lesson and not merely busy work, and (3) that what they write is valued. Using students' written responses in this way also provides teachers with a way to check informally (formative assessment) on students' understanding, as well as to gauge how best to proceed with the day's lesson. For example, students' answers to a prior knowledge question may tip off the teacher that more background information will need to be provided in order to teach the intended lesson successfully.

There also are ways to use this type of short writing activity during a class period and at the end of period instead of or in addition to doing so at the beginning of the period. These ways will be explored in the chapters that follow.

SOME THOUGHTS ON TAKING NOTES

Many teachers provide little or no guidance to students about taking notes in class. Some schools and some teachers offer sessions or entire classes on study skills that include note taking, but many of these classes are aimed at students who have trouble learning. Other students are left to fend for themselves. However, note taking can provide another vehicle for increasing students' writing for understanding, if teachers choose to use it as a writing strategy.

Taking notes "on the fly" as a lesson is being presented argues for jotting down words and phrases, not complete sentences or paragraphs. Students usually develop their own form of shorthand for this purpose. Where writing for understanding comes into focus is during the next (often omitted) stage, when students reread their jottings and write a summary. Karthigeyan Subramaniam (2008), an assistant professor of science education at Penn State Harrisburg, offers the following advice to teachers to improve students' note-taking skills and expand them to include writing for understanding:

> Model note-taking tools, skills, and cues. . . . Try to implement more introspective and active note-taking skills (discriminating between salient and non-salient notes to be written, summarizing notes from the textbook, comparing and contrasting facts, annotating drawings and sketches, giving students the independence to make their own notes), rather than passive note-taking skills (dictation, copying notes from the board or textbook). (np)

Note taking in this manner encourages students to use their notebooks, as Subramaniam (2008) says, as "repositories in which their content knowledge and writing work together to form meaning" (np). Taking notes with an eye to writing for understanding is another form of daily writing that is easy to integrate into the classroom routine and yet can have a powerful positive effect on increasing students' acquisition and understanding of content.

2

Developing Narrative Writing Assignments

This chapter and the next four focus on specific modes of writing. *Mode* in this context means a way or a manner of writing. Sometimes these modes also are referred to as *forms, types,* or *domains* of writing. Experts in composition identify modes in various ways, often depending on the context, for example, scholarly writing or journalistic writing. Each mode has a specific purpose.

Independent writers choose the mode in which to write by thinking carefully about the audience of readers they want to reach, the nature of the topic about which they want to write, and their purpose for writing. In developing questions or prompts to activate student learning and writing, teachers need to think about these same considerations. What kinds of higher level thinking do they want students to do? Which audience will engage and motivate students? What learning goals are students' thinking and writing intended to achieve?

Five modes to be considered in this book are identified as narrative, descriptive, expository, argumentative, and persuasive. Each mode merits its own chapter. This chapter begins with the first of these: narrative writing.

WHAT IS NARRATIVE WRITING?

Narrative writing tells a story or part of a story. Full-blown stories have a plot, a narrative *arc*, and include settings, actions, characters, conflict, and resolution. However, most of the writing done to improve content knowledge and understanding will not involve creating full-blown stories. Rather, students may be asked to write part of a story or an anecdote.

Albert Einstein famously declared that imagination is more important than knowledge. Using narrative writing with students changes the equation. Imagination stimulates knowledge acquisition and clarifies understanding. Stories that students read are staples in the instructional repertoire for teaching content—everything from episodes in history to principles in mathematics.

> **Types of Narrative Writing**
>
> - Stories—true-to-life and fiction
> - Anecdotes
> - Folktales and tall tales
> - Vignettes
> - Dramatic scripts

Far less often do teachers ask students to create their own stories. Yet narratives can be one of the most engaging forms for students to write. Such writing often is a natural motivator. One reason is that many stories tap personal experiences. Even though students usually are not expected to write lengthy stories, narrative writing often compels students to draw from within themselves. Children's book author Julius Lester (2004) says in his autobiography, "My books, all of them, have risen from the need to know who I am" (p. 104). Even spur-of-the-moment classroom narratives allow students to dip into this same inner well.

USING NARRATIVE WRITING

Narrative writing can be used for various purposes: activating prior knowledge, using concepts previously discussed, checking understanding, sharing information with peers, and so forth. If the narrative writing encourages students to personalize lesson content, then the act of writing will help make that content more meaningful and memorable. To illustrate this, let's assume that a science class is studying ecological footprints, a concept that involves measuring (or approximating) the effects of a person's energy-use choices on the environment. Instead of answering simple questions during the unit, students might be asked to write a story to illustrate what they are learning. A writing prompt might be stated something like this:

Write a story for your classmates in which one or more characters learn about ecological footprints and then make one or more lifestyle changes to reduce their negative effect on the Earth's ecosystem.

This example of using writing for understanding is based on one of the many energy lesson plans that can be found on the U.S. Department of

Energy website at www.eere.energy.gov/education/lessonplans. The lesson includes a survey that students complete online to assess their ecological footprint. Following is an example of a high school student's story based on having completed such a survey.

The ecological footprint results were startling! Pam's footprint measured 24.11 acres. That's 95.71 percent of the average North American's footprint, so she didn't feel too bad about that. Unfortunately, Americans use up more environmental resources than most people in the world. Her 24 acres were 139.47 percent of the world average. If everyone in the world consumed resources at the same rate as Pam, it would take more than six Earths to support everyone!

Pam immediately decided to make some changes. One was about driving alone. From now on, she would carpool to school. Maybe Joannie would like to ride with her, or she and Joannie could ride with Jennifer. The more, the better. That way they could all reduce their ecological footprints. Another way Pam decided to change was to turn off lights behind her at home. Her mom bugged her about that anyway, so maybe it was time she used less electricity. How much trouble was it to turn off a light? Pam was sure that if she really thought about it, she could find other ways to reduce her ecological footprint.

While the student's main character is Pam, the story might just as easily have been written in the first person, with "I" standing in for Pam. Joannie and Jennifer might be classmates or friends, or they might be fictional. These elements in students' stories will vary. Different students will take different approaches, all of which may be valid. The teacher need not be particularly concerned about the story form. It's the story content that is important. Has the writer correctly used or interpreted the information from the ecological footprint survey? Are Pam's conclusions and decisions reasonable, based on the survey results and other information presented in the lesson? What can this student's story about Pam and her friends teach other students in the class? As the teacher reads or listens to other students' stories, it also should be possible to judge whether the pace of instruction is too fast, too slow, or about right.

At the same time, perhaps an even more important assessment can be made—namely, as students listen to their classmates' stories, they can assess their own level of learning. Do they understand the material? How does their understanding compare with that of other students? Did they miss the point? Should they ask a question or seek help? Just as writing requires self-reflection, so too does critical reading and listening. This is why it is so valuable to share students' writing. Not only does sharing provide a motivating audience, it increases learning.

CLASS DIALOGUE

For writing to be meaningful both as an activity that engages student interest and as an instructional tool for increasing content knowledge and understanding, it needs to be shared in some way. Knowledge-building stories like the one about Pam's ecological footprint do not need to be collected and read by the teacher (though they can be), nor do they need to be marked or graded. If the teacher chooses to read and mark the stories, then the narrative writing may become less a way for students to build content knowledge and understandings and more a way for teachers to assess students' content mastery and then alter instruction accordingly. Both purposes are valid, but the focus here is on facilitating, rather than assessing, student learning. Judging appropriate pace of instruction informally will be a more efficient strategy and one that can be accomplished through the use of a class dialogue.

Students' writing can be published—printed, distributed, or posted. It can be shared with peers in pairs, triads, or small groups. Or it can be read aloud and discussed by the whole class. In the last case, sampling a few stories usually is sufficient. The teacher can ask students to volunteer to read their own stories, which works well in many classrooms, especially after the students have some experience using this process. If the teacher senses that students are not comfortable reading their own stories in front of the class, then students can exchange papers (with or without the writers' names on them). Then the teacher can ask the students to read whatever story they are holding.

Following is an example of a portion of a class dialogue that might take place after students have completed the writing assignment in the previous section.

Teacher: Yesterday we worked on ecological footprint surveys, and I asked you to write a short narrative about how a person might use the survey results to make lifestyle changes that would reduce his or her impact on the environment. Let's listen to two or three stories before we continue this lesson. Would someone volunteer to read?

Several hands go up, and the teacher asks Ellen to read her story, which is the sample in the previous section. Ellen reads, and then the teacher responds.

Teacher: Ellen, that was an excellent story. Thank you for reading it. Can someone else tell us why you think Ellen's character Pam chose carpooling as a way to decrease her ecological footprint?

Jeremy: (*Eagerly*) Pam drove to school by herself. Joannie and Jennifer probably did, too. That would waste energy.

Teacher: How would Pam have discovered this or come to this conclusion?

Jeremy: The footprint survey would show a high score for energy use on the question about driving habits.

Teacher: Exactly! Excellent answer, Jeremy. Let's check with Ellen. How did you get the idea for Pam to start carpooling, Ellen?

Ellen: I took the survey as if I were Pam. So when she put down that she drove to school by herself, she got a high number. I knew she could lower her footprint number by carpooling.

Teacher: That's a good strategy, Ellen. Can someone else suggest another way that Pam might lower the high score she got from driving alone? Maggie?

Maggie: If Pam was on the bus route, she could just take the bus instead of driving.

Teacher: You're right, Maggie. That's another strategy. Anyone else?

Sam: If she didn't live too far away, Pam could just walk. That would be even better.

Teacher: Why would that be better, Sam?

Sam: Well, riding the bus still means using energy. Bus exhaust contributes to pollution, but walking doesn't.

Teacher: Absolutely right, Sam. Thank you. Now let's hear another story. Who will volunteer?

This dialogue excerpt illustrates some key components for successfully engaging students in classroom conversations about writing for understanding. Note that the teacher is not concerned about story structure or plot development or any of the typical writing elements that would be discussed in a writing class. The teacher's focus is on content.

Following are some ways that this teacher directs the class dialogue. They can serve as general guidelines:

- Acknowledge the story and thank the author or reader.
- Check interpretations and seek clarification from the writer as needed. For example, when Jeremy interprets the story, the teacher turns to Ellen, the writer, to check whether Jeremy's idea jibes with hers.
- Draw other students into the dialogue by asking them to respond to elements of the story.
- Ask follow-up questions when appropriate. For example, when Sam says that walking would be even better than riding the bus, the teacher asks Sam to expand on his point.

What if a student reads a story that does not meet the assignment? How then might the dialogue proceed? These general guidelines still hold. However, two of the guidelines become more important. One is checking interpretations and seeking clarification from the writer. Did the student writer misunderstand the idea of writing a story? Or is the student uncertain about the lesson content that is to be used as the basis for the story—in this case, obtaining and interpreting the results of an ecological footprint survey? The other key guideline is drawing other students into the dialogue. For example, the teacher might ask,

"Can someone suggest how a character might act if he or she got a score of X percent on the ecological footprint survey?"

"How might the main character in this story respond to the challenge to lower his or her negative effect on the ecosystem?"

In other words, the teacher should enlist the assistance of other students—critical listeners—to suggest ways to improve the story and thus, at the same time, to improve the writer's understanding of content.

Chapter 7 provides more information about how to conduct class dialogues and other writing discussions that help students construct meaning and master content.

USING NARRATIVE WRITING TO BUILD CONTENT VOCABULARY

All subjects use some specialized vocabulary that students are expected to learn. Many teachers have found, often by trial and error, that most students do not acquire new vocabulary without specific effort. That is, they do not tend to learn new words merely by reading or hearing them. This leads to vocabulary lists, and students may be admonished to write the words multiple times, say and spell them aloud, and use them in sentences. These are fairly standard vocabulary-building procedures, and for some students they work well. But the real test of vocabulary mastery is whether the student can correctly use the words in meaningful contexts.

Narrative writing can be a means to help students integrate new content-specific terms into their internal dictionaries. Following is a sample prompt inspired by lessons in *We the People: The Citizen and the Constitution* (2009), a civics textbook published by the Center for Civic Education (www.civiced.org):

Write a short narrative set in the American colonies in the late 1600s and use at least five of the following terms. Make sure that each term is used correctly and meaningfully.

Charter

Constituents

Covenant

Indentured servants

Magistrate

Servitude

Suffrage

Here is a sample student response:

The only way my brother Aaron and I could get to the New World was to sign on to become **indentured servants** to a **magistrate** in the Virginia colony. John Watson was his name. He had a **charter** to the land we would farm for him. We knew that it meant a life of **servitude** for several years and we wouldn't have **suffrage**. But that was okay because it meant we would get to live in America and someday make our fortune.

This response is minimally successful. The requisite five terms are used correctly. But it is unclear whether the student has more than a superficial command of the terms' meanings. One way to help students improve narrative responses like this one is to talk through improvements in a class dialogue. Such discussion can be facilitated by projecting the story on a transparency so that changes can be displayed as they are made. In high-tech classrooms, the same technique can be employed by projecting a computer word-processing file onto a screen and adding changes at the keyboard.

The teacher should direct the students to read the story silently and then ask, "How can we add to this story so that someone who doesn't know these new vocabulary terms will understand them in context?"

Following is the story after the class additions, which are italicized:

The only way my brother Aaron and I could get to the New World was to sign on to become **indentured servants**, *which meant we would be almost like slaves. We agreed to work for* ~~to~~ a **magistrate** in the Virginia colony. *Judge* John Watson was his name. *He held court for minor crimes in a small town.* He *also* had a **charter**, *which was a grant from the colonial government,* to ~~the~~ land *that* we would farm for him. We knew that it meant a life of **servitude**, *serving the judge as his farmhands* for several years, and we wouldn't have **suffrage**, *which meant we would not be allowed to vote until we became citizens after our indenture.* But that was okay because it meant we would get to live in America and someday make our fortune.

This exercise demonstrates the importance of writing for an audience—and helping students consider an audience as they formulate their narrative. A proactive approach in writing prompts such as the one for this assignment is to include consideration of an audience in the prompt rather than leaving it to the students' interpretation. In the original prompt when the teacher asks students to make sure that each term is used *meaningfully*, the teacher's intent was for students to write so that a reader unfamiliar with the terms will be able to understand them. That idea needs to be made explicit for students. Students may not readily understand the implication. The solution is to cue them as to audience expectations in the prompt. Therefore a revised prompt might look like this:

Write a short narrative set in the American colonies in the late 1600s and use at least five of the following terms. Make sure that each term is used correctly and meaningfully. *Write so that someone who doesn't know these new vocabulary terms will understand them in context.*

SAMPLE NARRATIVE WRITING QUESTIONS AND PROMPTS

Mature writers often draw from several content areas regardless of the mode in which they write. The same will be true for much of the writing that students are asked to do. In this chapter, for example, the narrative prompt about using an ecological footprint survey comes from a science lesson, but it presumes at least a basic understanding of percentages, a math concept. The vocabulary prompt was drawn from a civics lesson, but it could just as easily be used in a class on American history. Similar vocabulary-related prompts could work in most subjects.

Many writing prompts also can cross levels. Similar information can be found in upper elementary, middle, and high school classes, although the content differs in depth, complexity, and sophistication. In instances when a question or prompt will work equally well at various levels, it may be only the depth of the students' writing that differs.

To conclude this chapter and the next four, sample prompts are clustered into four broad categories:

Effective Writing Questions and Prompts

- Ask students to use prior knowledge and new content knowledge.
- Suggest or specify an audience of readers, real or imaginary.
- Encourage creativity.
- In some instances, build content vocabulary knowledge.

Mathematics and Science

Social Studies (history, civics, psychology, sociology, economics)

The Arts (visual arts, music, theater, dance)

Physical Education (fitness, health)

These categories conform to the National Standards (see Kendall & Marzano, 1996). Language-based content areas (language arts, foreign languages) are omitted because those classes already will (or should) emphasize writing for various purposes, including writing for understanding. The purpose of these prompts is to suggest approaches that teachers can adapt for writing prompts based on the content knowledge they want their students to acquire.

Mathematics and Science

- Imagine that you and a friend are going to plant a vegetable garden this summer on a plot measuring eight by ten feet. After reading the seed packet, you calculate that your garden will yield between eight and twelve carrots in each square foot of soil. Write a story for your classmates in which you and the friend discuss your garden plans and how many carrots you expect to harvest and to share equally.
- Write a story for someone two or three grades before yours in which two or more characters discuss examples of how trial-and-error thinking has propelled the course of scientific discovery or technological invention.

Social Studies

- Put yourself into the scene when Patrick Henry delivered his famous "Give Me Liberty or Give Me Death" speech on March 23, 1775. Write a story as if you were a newspaper reporter covering the event.
- You are Charles Lindbergh in the cockpit of *The Spirit of St. Louis* on May 21, 1927, and you have just sighted the Eiffel Tower. Write a narrative about your feelings as you are about to land in Paris, the first person to fly nonstop across the Atlantic Ocean, and how history will see this accomplishment.

The Arts

- Imagine that you are sitting in a café with Pablo Picasso. He tells you about his plans to create a mural that he will call simply *Guernica*. Write a dialogue in which Picasso discusses his reasons for creating this painting.

- Write a short narrative set in a composer's studio and use at least five of the following terms. Make sure that each term is used correctly and meaningfully, and write so that a reader who does not know these terms will understand them in context.

Beat

Cadence

Chord

Chord progression

Chromatic scale

Consonance

Dissonance

Physical Education

- Create a dialogue in which two or three characters discuss basic volleyball rules and scoring strategies. Write so that a student in elementary school who is just learning the game will understand the basics from your story.
- Write a story for your classmates in which an individual has completed a nutrition survey, obtained a poor score, and now wants to improve how he or she eats. How might your character think about the survey and respond positively?

3

Developing Descriptive Writing Assignments

Modes of writing are seldom *pure*, or wholly defined by a particular type of writing. For example, most narrative writing, which was discussed in Chapter 2, includes at least some basic description. What would a story be, after all, without a sense of place or without characters? Most of the narrative writing that students do to increase content understanding does not depend on explicit description. Anecdotes, for instance, typically allow the reader to envision the characters and the setting based on the situation, rather than outright description. Similarly, dialogues, such as those found in scripts, rely on what a character says and how it is said to create a visual image for the reader or listener. But scripts can include explicit description as notes to the director, or reader, about how scenes and characters should look and sound.

When it comes to modes of writing, any label—narrative, descriptive—simply indicates the dominant or intended mode. In this chapter, the mode under the magnifying glass is descriptive writing.

WHAT IS DESCRIPTIVE WRITING?

The word *describe* comes from the Latin *describere,* meaning to "copy off or write down." In modern parlance, it has come to mean to create a word picture, literally to write down what you see so that the reader can see it as you do. Common forms that students are asked to write are the sketch and the descriptive essay. Both of these are valuable tools to increase content knowledge and understanding through writing.

Most descriptive writing is intended to create a clear impression by using details. The impression may be objective or subjective. For example, an objective description of a building might stress facts, such as the number of floors or windows, the building's structural composition (wood, steel, and so on), surface materials (brick or stone), proportion, architectural style, and other characteristics. A subjective description of the same building probably would include some of these factual details but also might incorporate the writer's personal thoughts—details of another sort—such as how the writer connects with the building's history or how he or she feels when the sun strikes the building in a certain way.

Description is not limited to static scenes. Teachers also ask students to describe events and processes, such as the interplay of athletes in a competition, chemical reactions in a science experiment, or the actions of individuals and groups during a political protest.

The most common way to describe a person, object, scene, event, or process is through the visual sense. Vision is the dominant human sense. Indeed, we talk about description mainly in visual terms. *Sketch*, for example, parallels the word's use in visual arts, where a sketch is a purely visual rendering of an observed subject in pencil, ink, paint, or some other medium. A sketch in writing is a description. Most often that description will be predominantly visual in character. However, effective descriptive writing relies on solid, sensory details, and the sketch or descriptive essay will be richer, fuller, and more explicit if students are taught to observe and to imagine beyond the purely visual.

USING DESCRIPTIVE WRITING

Observation is a learned skill and one that teachers of all subjects should nurture in their students. Observation involves activities such as examining types of mathematical equations, noting the results of science experiments, seeing patterns in musical scores or works of visual art, or finding ways that historical themes unfold and repeat. Observation is a means not only to accumulate knowledge but also to *grow* existing knowledge and understanding—to *construct* new knowledge in constructivist terms.

Of course, not everything will lend itself to multisensory description. Straightforward mathematical equations, for example, usually are expressed visually as numbers or objects that represent numbers. A writer might

Sensory Details

- How does the subject (object, person, event, action) look?
- What sounds are associated with the subject?
- What are the touch sensations, such as texture?
- Are there identifiable aromas or odors?
- What about taste sensations?

describe an apple pie by referring to how it looks, smells, and tastes, but it would not make sense to do the same for the mathematical concept of pi (π). On the other hand, a description of a chemical reaction might be incomplete if expressed only in visual terms. For example, two clear substances might be mixed without an observable change in color or clarity. But what about odor? Does the new mixture smell different than the separate original liquids? How does the mixture feel? Is it slimy or sticky? In this case, the visual sense would be subordinate to smell and touch.

Effective observation and description draw on all applicable senses, whether that means one, two, or all five. The key to working with students on using descriptive writing to increase content knowledge and understanding is to help them use all available sensory input to shape their descriptive writing.

A strategy that works well to expand and strengthen students' observation skills is one called "sense exploration" (Walling, 1978, 2006). A simple chart, such as the Sense Exploration Template in Figure 3.1, can help students consciously employ all their senses. The strategy is to chart descriptive words or phrases—concrete details—that subsequently can be used to develop a written description. Following is a sample prompt:

You have been reading about lighter-than-air travel and have seen a film clip of the famous *Hindenburg* disaster in 1937. Put yourself on the ground, witnessing the *Hindenburg* as it approaches the mooring point at Lakehurst Naval Air Station. Suddenly the giant airship bursts into flames. Describe the scene by first charting sense observations. Make sure to use all five senses. Then develop a short sketch.

Figure 3.1   Sense Exploration Template

Sight	Hearing	Smell	Touch	Taste

This prompt or a slight adaptation might be used in a number of lessons, including

- Hydrogen and helium properties (science)
- Development of air travel (science, history)
- Rise of Nazism prior to World War II (history)

The film clip of the *Hindenburg* disaster referred to in the prompt, complete with the famous radio commentary, can be accessed online through YouTube (www.youtube.com/watch?v=F54rqDh2mWA) or through Wikipedia (en.wikipedia.org/wiki/Hindenburg_disaster).

Figure 3.2 shows an example of the notes in a sense exploration template for a description of the *Hindenburg* disaster. Following is one student's description based on those notes.

> The giant German zeppelin *Hindenburg* was like a man-made cloud as it floated toward the mooring mast. The wind was gusty and wet. It had been raining earlier and the air smelled like it could start up again anytime. I put my hand up to keep my hat from blowing off. The wind made it hard to hear the propeller motors that were being used to hold the airship steady as it came in. All of a sudden there was a terrific explosion and flames shot out. I jumped at the sound. In seconds, the whole zeppelin was a ball of fire. The heat and smoke pushed down. I could feel it on my face. I was choking and tasting the hot ashes. Then I ran with the others. Some people were screaming. The groaning of the crumpling metal frame, the roar of the flames, and the screams and cries felt as though they were pushing me, pushing all of us. We ran to get out from under the falling inferno.

Figure 3.2 Sense Exploration Template: Hindenburg Disaster

Sight	Hearing	Smell	Touch	Taste
Giant zeppelin	Wind gusts	Rain	Wind—hat about to blow off	Hot ashes
Man-made cloud	Propeller motors	Smoke	Heat from fire	Choking smoke
Ball of flames	Explosion		Wind and heat pushing me	
Crumpling metal frame	Crackling flames			
People running	Human screams and cries			

This type of description combines observation and imagination. A reasonable question is, does this type of writing really improve students' understanding of content? The answer is a resounding yes. When students describe people, places, events, processes, and the like, they are developing observation skills (even when such observation is fictionalized), learning how to use concrete details, and to order ideas in logical ways. As this strategy is internalized, it supports both active and subconscious construction of new knowledge and understanding.

This particular type of descriptive writing is similar to what Rothstein, Rothstein, and Lauber (2007) call *personification*, in which the writer puts himself or herself into the shoes of another, such as a historical figure or, as in this example, a witness to an important event. Rothstein et al. (2007) write,

> The ability to role-play brings about the ability to understand what it is like, as stated succinctly in American Indian folklore, to "walk the path in someone else's moccasins." . . . [Students] can further develop an understanding of motivation and dedication by interactive writing, a process of making the person that one is studying come alive. (p. 206)

Making the *what's* and *who's* that students are studying "come alive" also is a powerful motivator for student learning. This type of descriptive writing is a highly effective instructional strategy, particularly when used before or during a lesson in science, social studies, or the arts. At these times the writing task tends to propel the lesson, adding energy and increasing students' motivation to learn.

DESCRIBING PROCESSES

Physical education activities and laboratory sciences are especially appropriate for process descriptions. Describing in a journal or log book what happened during a sports play or science experiment are, or should be, standard instructional strategies. Often, however, process descriptions take place in verbal interactions and are not extended into written form. While process discussions (sometimes termed, á la science, *dissections*) of plays in football, basketball, soccer, baseball, and other sports are useful, they tend to be fleeting, and their instructional value can be similarly ephemeral. Putting how-it-happened process observations into written form *and then* discussing what various students saw can enrich analysis and deepen understanding and memory. This is all the more powerful when students' observations vary, which can foster detailed, nuanced debates that require students to examine subjective and objective realities.

One strategy that many science teachers use to good advantage is a project or experiment journal or log book, in which students describe processes and observations. Ongoing log entries may range from weather notes about daily temperature, wind speed and direction, cloud conditions, relative humidity, and the like to observations of plant, mold, or crystal growth over a period of days, weeks, or months. Such journaling often is not descriptive writing but merely note taking. However, these notes can be summarized or synthesized into elaborated written descriptions. For example, Figure 3.3 is an excerpt from a student's log book at the start of a crystal-growing experiment. Following are a prompt and a response based on the log notes:

Prompt: We started our crystal-growing experiment about a week ago. Use the information you have recorded in your log book to write a one- or two-paragraph description to share with your classmates. Tell what you have done so far and what you have observed.

Response: I started like everyone else by mixing up 30 grams of potash alum in 200 milliliters of hot water. The solution was milky. I ran it through a filter into a clean beaker and put the beaker into the project cabinet. This was on Monday, January 14, at 9:30 a.m. The next day in class I saw six small crystals in the bottom of the beaker. They were white or transparent. I picked out the largest one and tied a really fine nylon fishing line to it. I tied the other end to a pencil that I balanced on top of a new beaker. The crystal hung down into the solution that I poured into the new beaker. Then I marked the level of the solution on the side of the beaker. I covered it with a filter paper and put it in the project cabinet.

On Monday, January 21, I saw that the crystal was bigger and had three branches that were shorter than the main crystal. The main crystal and the branches had smooth faces. I counted 15 in all. Mostly the crystal was clear, but the center was whitish. The crystal measured about one and a half centimeters long. The solution had evaporated down about two centimeters.

Figure 3.3   Crystal Growing Log Book Excerpt

Date/Time	Describe What You Did. Problems? Solutions?	Crystal Characteristics
Jan. 14 9:30 a.m.	Put 30 g of potash alum in 200 ml of hot water. Filtered water into clean beaker. Covered new beaker and put into project cabinet.	No crystals. Water was milky.
Jan. 15 9:30 a.m.	Uncovered beaker and saw small crystals. Poured remaining solution into clean beaker.	Six small crystals of different sizes grew on the bottom of the beaker. White or clear crystals.

Date/Time	Describe What You Did. Problems? Solutions?	Crystal Characteristics
	Picked largest crystal out with a clean spoon. Tied fishing line to the crystal and to a pencil. Hung the crystal in the solution in the new beaker. Marked level of solution. Covered new beaker with filter paper. Put project into cabinet.	
Jan. 21 **9:30 a.m.**	Measured the solution. It had evaporated about 2 cm. Measure the crystal. It had grown to about 1½ cm at the longest.	Original crystal grew three new branches that were shorter but had smooth faces. Counted 15 faces in all. Crystal was mostly clear with a cloudy, whitish center where the branches met.

CLASS DIALOGUE

As suggested in the previous chapter, an effective follow-up to writing is a brief class dialogue. Following is an example based on the previous writing prompt:

Teacher: Let's sample some of the descriptions you wrote based on what has been happening in your crystal experiments. Who would like to volunteer to read theirs?

Several hands go up, and the teacher asks Chad to read his description, which is the example in the previous section. Chad reads, and then the teacher responds.

Teacher: Chad, that was a pretty thorough description. Thank you for reading it. It sounds as though your experiment is going well. Just one point: I think I heard you refer to the crystal *faces*. Did you mean *facets*?

Chad: Oh, right. Facets. I couldn't think of the right word.

Teacher: While we're on the subject of facets, can someone tell us the difference between the facets on your crystals and, say, the facets on a diamond?

A few hands go up. The teacher calls on Bethany.

Bethany: Our crystals just grow their facets. The facets on a diamond have to be cut by a jeweler.

Teacher: Excellent answer, Bethany. We'll talk more about that later. Now, let's hear another description or two, and then we can discuss where to go from here with the crystal project.

As in the dialogue from Chapter 2, the teacher samples the descriptions by asking various students to read what they have written, validates the students' efforts, makes or elicits corrections, and then uses the writing exercise as a transition to the next part of the lesson. Dialogues of this type are not intended to be long discussions.

TRANSLATING MATHEMATICS

There was an apocryphal story making the e-mail rounds recently about a fellow who went to a fast-food restaurant to order a half-dozen chicken nuggets. The teenage clerk responded, "Sorry, sir, we only sell them in orders of three, six, nine, or twelve."

"So," the fellow responded, "I can't order a half-dozen, but I can order six?"

"Right," said the clerk.

The fellow shook his head and ordered six.

Students who have difficulty learning mathematics, whether in a math class or as math is applied in other subjects, often respond that it is like learning a foreign language. Indeed, the manipulation of numbers, relationships, equations—even definitions of terms such as *dozen*—is like working in a different language. Consequently, it often makes sense to view writing about mathematics as *translation*—that is, translating the language of numbers into the language of words. This can be a highly effective way to help students struggling with mathematical concepts and computations. It also can provide a steppingstone to tackling word problems, which seem to evoke nearly universal dread.

Following is a prompt at the level of basic description:

Describe in a short paragraph the steps you use to convert the fraction one-fourth to a percentage. Make sure you describe each step so that a classmate could read your description and follow it easily.

A response might be as follows:

I take the four in one-fourth and divide it into 100. The answer is twenty-five. Then I take the one times twenty-five. The answer is still twenty-five, so one-fourth equals 25 percent.

At higher levels, writing about mathematics includes not only description but also analysis and interpretation. The label sometimes associated with this more advanced approach is quantitative writing, which "forces students to contemplate the meaning of numbers, to understand where the numbers come from and how they are presented" (see Science Education Resource Center's Website at serc.carleton.edu/sp/library/quantitative_writing/what.html). Chapter 4, which centers on expository writing, will expand on this topic.

GIVING DIRECTIONS

Most people think of description mainly in terms of observation and reflection. But giving directions also is a common form of descriptive writing. Take the example in the previous section. The prompt might easily be rewritten as follows:

Write step-by-step directions in which you describe for a classmate how to convert the fraction one-fourth to a percentage.

A response might be as follows:

First, take the four in the fraction and divide it into one hundred. The answer should be twenty-five. Next, multiply twenty-five by the one in the fraction. The answer is the percentage.

If vocabulary-building is added, a slightly more sophisticated response might be:

First, take the *denominator* (four) and divide it into 100 percent. The answer should be twenty-five. Then multiply twenty-five by the *numerator* (one) to get the percentage, which will be 25 percent.

A couple of points are worth mentioning. First, notice that in this prompt and the previous one, the student is asked to describe a specific conversion, not to describe the process of converting fractions to percentages generally. Students should be able to do both, but whether to proceed from the specific to the general or from the general to the specific often is a matter of preference, both the teacher's preferred instructional sequence and the student's preferred learning sequence.

Second, many directions are given as numbered lists. However, writing lists blunts the value of descriptive writing as a strategy for increasing content knowledge and understanding. In fact, one strategy that can be helpful in teaching students how to write descriptively and encouraging them to write descriptive prose is to give students an existing numbered set of directions and ask them to rewrite the list into one or two descriptive paragraphs. The numbered directions can be anything from how to fold an origami crane to how to set a digital clock.

Giving directions using descriptive writing also can incorporate sense exploration. A favorite lesson that I have used with middle and high school students is designed to help students think beyond the merely visual. This is a good warm-up exercise, regardless of subject matter. The prompt goes like this:

A visitor will be coming to our classroom. Write one or two paragraphs giving this visitor directions from the main door of the school to this classroom. By the way, the visitor is blind. Your directions will be read to this person. Use the appropriate columns of a sense exploration template to note important sensory guideposts to include in your directions.

This assignment is best complemented by an in-school "field trip," during which students trace the route that the visitor will take before writing their directions. Students sometimes work in teams, with one student blindfolded and describing sounds, textures, steps, smells, and so on, while the other student acts as guide and notetaker.

SAMPLE DESCRIPTIVE WRITING QUESTIONS AND PROMPTS

Descriptive writing may well be the form of writing that students are called on to do most often. Accurate observation is a skill that teachers of every subject want their students to learn. Descriptive writing relies on observation and concrete details. The more that students are asked to expand and refine their observations through detailed sketches and descriptive essays, including directions, the greater their power of observation will become.

Remind students to use

- All five senses whenever possible
- Concrete details
- Sequence words to indicate order of events

Following are sample prompts that teachers can use as models to develop their own questions and prompts for descriptive writing that will increase students' acquisition of content knowledge and understanding.

Mathematics and Science

- Solve the equation $5x - 5 = 7x - 19$. Then describe for your classmates in one or two paragraphs the steps you took to solve for x.
- You recently completed a distillation experiment using a cola soft drink. The resulting distillate was clear liquid. Describe the equipment and the process that you used in this experiment. Also describe

your results. In what ways was the clear liquid distillate similar to and different from the cola? Write your descriptive essay so that a student who takes this class next year will be able to replicate your experiment.

Social Studies

- We have been studying trench warfare conditions that the military on both sides of the conflict faced during World War I. Imagine yourself as a soldier in a trench. Describe what that experience might have been like. Use a sense exploration template to prepare yourself for writing so that your sketch includes all five senses.
- Describe the actual Mason-Dixon Line as it was surveyed in the 1760s by Charles Mason and Jeremiah Dixon. Write so that a reader could accurately draw the Mason-Dixon Line on a map based solely on your description.

The Arts

- Write one or two short paragraphs describing the following scenery-painting techniques. Write so that a classmate who has never worked on stage scenery will understand how to use these techniques based on your description.

  Dry-brush

  Dribble

  Spatter

  Criss-cross

  Daub

  Scumble

  Wash

- As you watched the cello demonstration yesterday, you were asked to observe and make notes about several things: (1) the position of the cello, (2) the posture of the cellist, and (3) the positions of the cellist's arms and hands. Briefly describe your observations and be prepared to share your writing with the class.

Physical Education

- We have all seen the video clip of the winning touchdown, but did we all see the same thing? Write a sketch describing what you saw as accurately as you can. Be prepared to read your description aloud.
- Briefly describe the food pyramid. Be sure to include examples of food groups and specific foods in the various levels of the pyramid. Write this description as though you were going to read it to a parent or other relative who often makes meals for you.

4

Developing Expository Writing Assignments

Chapter 3 opens with the statement that modes of writing are seldom *pure*, meaning that the various types of writing are given labels that denote a dominant or intended mode. This certainly is true of expository writing. Indeed, some writing experts include descriptive writing under the expository umbrella, particular descriptions of processes and directions. However, such nuances may be confusing to students, and they do little to further the goal of increasing and enhancing content knowledge and understanding.

It is helpful to identify descriptive writing as concerned mainly with *what* questions, while expository writing is concerned mainly with *how* and *why* questions. Sketches and descriptive essays, including (in some cases) directions and descriptions of processes, focus on details that make up a sensory *whole*. But such details do not explain why or how the scene or process works or came to be. The how's and why's are essential to expository writing.

WHAT IS EXPOSITORY WRITING?

Expository writing *exposes*, or reveals, information by taking description one or more steps further in terms of elaboration. *Expose*, however, can be

> **Expository** writing *explains*. It goes beyond simple description to instruct or to clarify. When students engage in expository writing, they are able to clarify understandings about new content.

a limiting term, for expository writing does more than merely display a subject; it explains the subject. Thus *explain, instruct,* and *clarify* are terms associated with expository writing in addition to *describe*.

Consider the idea behind expositions such as the World's Fairs of the 1980s or the Expos of the 1990s and 2000s. These events, like their early predecessors—the Great Exhibition in London's Crystal Palace in 1851, the Paris International of 1855, or the 1876 Centennial Exposition in Philadelphia—were intended not only as opportunities for nations to "show and tell," but as events at which the world's citizens could learn about the latest scientific and technological advances. The expositions *explained* how new inventions worked and *instructed* fairgoers in the art and science behind the technology that was destined to change the way people communicated, traveled, washed their clothes, or grew their vegetables. In concrete ways, these and many other expositions have been and continue to be, in essence, about increasing public knowledge and understanding.

Move this metaphor into the classroom: Expository writing helps students increase content knowledge and understanding by putting them into the teaching role. Writing to explain—an event, a process—allows students take on the role of "exposer," or teacher. There's an adage that if you want to learn a subject really well, try teaching it to someone else. That's what expository writing accomplishes for students.

A caveat (admittedly tongue-in-cheek): Antoine de Saint-Exupery's Little Prince (in the 1943 children's book of that name) comments, "Grown-ups never understand anything for themselves, and it is tiresome for children to be always and forever explaining things to them." One hopes, however, that properly managed expository writing assignments will empower and motivate students rather than wear them out. The Little Prince's advice should be taken as a reminder to teachers to vary assignments among the modes.

USING EXPOSITORY WRITING

To use expository writing assignments effectively, teachers will find it helpful to focus on three sets of skills that are elemental in exposition:

- Defining and classifying
- Comparing and contrasting
- Showing reasons, causes, and effects

Defining and classifying. Like describing, defining relies on using concrete details. But where a description usually is explicit about specifics, definition may be general—and generalizable—using specifics as underpinning and examples. For instance, science students might be asked to distinguish between what happens (a description) in a specific laboratory experiment, such as distilling a clear liquid from a cola soft drink, and how distillation works as a basic laboratory process (a definition). A satisfactory definition of distillation will be general in character and will be applicable, or generalizable, to experiments using a variety of liquids, not just a cola soft drink.

Writing a workable definition can be challenging, which makes definition assignments all the better as a strategy to stimulate careful and creative thinking about content. Such thought deepens content knowledge and understanding. Keep in mind that these assignments ask students to create definitions, not merely to find them in a dictionary or some other text or simply to use them. Following are a prompt and two responses to illustrate how writing a definition might be used in an ecology lesson.

Prompt: Yesterday we took your individual surveys of the contents of your family's trash cans and merged them into an overall description of things that people typically throw away. Based on that description how would you define *trash?* Write your definition in one or two sentences.

Response 1: Trash is stuff that people throw away.

Response 2: Trash is worthless things that people want to get rid of, such as empty soda cans, bicycle tires, plastic milk jugs, and banana peels.

A follow-up class dialogue after students have read these two responses aloud might go something like this:

Teacher: What key characteristic do we look for in a good definition?

Several hands go up, and students voice their ideas. The teacher hones in on June's answer.

June: I think the most important thing is for a definition to work in all cases.

Teacher: Which of these two definitions does that?

June: The first one. It's the most general.

Teacher: But isn't it too short? Why not the second one? That sounds pretty typical to me. Brian, you have your hand up.

Brian: It might be typical here or even in a lot of places. But maybe people in Africa throw away different things.

Teacher: So what you're saying is that a good definition is generalizable. We're trying to define trash, not just American trash.

Brian: Right. The second one is really more like a description than a definition.

Teacher: That's a good point, Brian. What about the idea in the second definition that trash is worthless? Is that true?

A few hands go up. The teacher calls on Shirley.

Shirley: Just because someone throws something away doesn't make it worthless. Isn't there a saying that one person's trash is another person's treasure?

Teacher: Excellent answer, Shirley. Let's talk about some of these treasures in terms of recycling.

In fact, the first definition in this example is essentially a typical dictionary definition of *trash* as "discarded matter." The point that the teacher is getting across is that an effective definition is broadly applicable.

This particular class dialogue provides a logical transition for this lesson, moving students from thinking about trash in general to considering the topic of recycling. This transition also introduces another aspect of definition: classification.

After further discussion about local waste disposal policies, for instance, students might be asked to summarize their understanding of trash and recycling in their community. A writing prompt asking students to explain how local regulations classify recyclable matter might look like this:

Write a paragraph that you could include in a letter or an e-mail to a person living in another community. Explain our town's recycling program. Identify and give examples of at least four categories of trash that can be recycled in our community.

Following is a sample student response:

In our town, the trash we want to recycle is collected every other week along with the other trash. We just have to put the recycling in different bins or boxes. We can recycle glass, paper, plastic, and metal containers among other things. Glass can be jars (without lids) or bottles. Paper can be newspapers, magazines, or paper bags. Plastic can be milk jugs, laundry soap bottles, or soda bottles (without caps). Metal can be cans from food or soda.

Comparing and contrasting. Classification also is a gateway into comparing (noting similarities) and contrasting (finding differences). The word *compare* often is used to elicit both similarities and differences, but in the present context it is used in a more limited sense of seeking similarities.

Definitions have two aspects. The first is the more general, called *denotation*, the literal meaning. The second, *connotation*, refers to ideas or feelings that a word evokes beyond its literal meaning. For example, consider words that essentially mean *house*, such as *hovel, hut, shack, mansion,* and *manor*. All of these denote types of houses, but their connotations vary. The connotation of *mansion* (a large stately house) is very different from that of *hut* (a small, simple house) and *hovel* (a dirty, poorly built house).

For the ecology lesson, a writing prompt might be framed to get students to compare and contrast classifications of trash by considering connotations associated with other words that are used to refer to trash:

Think about your definition of *trash* and then write one-sentence definitions for the following terms: *refuse, waste, garbage, rubbish, litter,* and *junk.* Next consider these two questions: Do all of these terms mean the same thing? How are they similar to or different from one another?

Defining, classifying, comparing, and contrasting are applicable not only to writing about vocabulary words. They also call for higher level thinking when applied to complex concepts. In art history, for example, expository writing assignments might ask students to consider historical styles and related artists. Following are three sample prompts:

Definition: Two of the art movements that characterized the eighteenth and nineteenth centuries were Romanticism and Impressionism. Briefly define each of these movements and summarize their main themes in a short essay.

Classification: Classify each of the following artists according to whether his or her work would be seen as Romantic or Impressionistic. Does any artist not fit either movement? Be prepared to read your essay to the class.

Eugène Delacroix	Claude Monet	Pierre Auguste Renoir
Berthe Morisot	J. M. W. Turner	Francisco Goya

Compare and contrast: In what ways are the painting styles of Francisco Goya and Pierre Auguste Renoir similar? In what ways are they different? Write two paragraphs, one for comparison and the other for contrast.

Defining, classifying, comparing, and contrasting styles and practitioners are broadly applicable. Consider, for example, political parties and candidates in history or current events, music and composers or musicians, choreographers and their work, sports (British rugby and American football, for instance) and team play (types of offense and defense), and scientific beliefs and practices. Every subject is rich with opportunities for students to use exposition to deepen their content knowledge and understanding.

Showing reasons, causes, and effects. Another set of skills in expository writing requires the student writer to dig into the why's of actions or processes. These skills complement the other sets of skills. Let's go back to a math writing prompt from the previous chapter. Remember, that one involved giving directions:

Write a step-by-step description in which you describe for a classmate how to convert the fraction one-fourth to a percentage.

An easy way to expand this assignment from description to exposition is to ask for a definition of *percentage* and reasons for the operations involved in the conversion. An expanded prompt might look something like this:

Define *percentage* and then write a step-by-step description for a classmate, explaining how to convert the fraction one-fourth to a percentage and why each step is necessary.

The student answer from Chapter 3 is shown below with additions in italics that respond to the expanded prompt:

A percentage is a proportion stated in one-hundredths. That means a "whole" contains 100 percent, just like a dollar equals 100 cents. To make one-fourth into a percentage, you first take the four in the fraction and divide it into 100. *The fraction means that you have one of four parts of a "whole."* The answer should be twenty-five. Next, multiply twenty-five by the one in the fraction *because you only have one-fourth. If you had three-fourths, you would multiply twenty-five by three.* The answer *(1 x 25)* is the percentage, *or twenty-five percent. You can check this if you think about the dollar. One-fourth of a dollar is called a "quarter," which is worth twenty-five cents.*

In the solving of complicated mathematical equations, the mantra often is, "Show your work!" Using expository writing in this way provides another way for students to show their work—that is, to show the reasoning behind the operations.

Much the same can be said of showing causes and effects, but cause-and-effect reasoning can be a special case, as will be discussed later in this chapter.

CLASS DIALOGUE

The student answer in the previous section offers an exemplary focus for a follow-up class dialogue that might proceed something like this:

Teacher: It sounds as though we agree that Jim's response *(above)* to the writing prompt is a good one. What makes it good? Why do you think a student who is learning how to convert fractions to percentages would find Jim's answer easy to understand?

Several hands go up, and the teacher calls on Ginny.

Ginny: The definition is simple and applies in all cases.

Teacher: Right, Ginny. The definition is generalizable. What else? Gary?

Gary: I think the example of the dollar really helps make percentage easy to understand.

Teacher: Excellent answer, Gary. A concrete example helps make the meaning clear. Jim, why did you choose this particular example?

Jim: It just seemed logical. "Cent" and "percent" fit the definition, with 100 cents in a whole dollar and 100 percent in a "whole" something-or-other.

Teacher: Good reasoning, Jim. Did anyone use a different example?

As in previous class dialogues the teacher validates the students' writing and responses, taking opportunities to reinforce learned content, such as when the teacher in this dialogue restates Ginny's point that the definition "applies in all cases." A logical continuation of this dialogue would be to discuss various examples that other students used and whether those examples were effective.

Class dialogues in the context of writing for understanding necessarily focus on content rather than form. However, content and form cannot be wholly separated. The information that goes into this expository writing assignment, or any other piece of writing, shapes the written work. Verbal exchanges between the teacher and the students help keep attention on the content.

That said, in some cases it may be useful to display students' writing rather than asking students to read aloud, for example, when a longer composition results from a more complex prompt. Displays of work can be done by scanning the written text and projecting the electronic file using an LCD, DLP, or similar projector. Another way to display students' compositions for discussion is by copying the written text onto a transparency and using an overhead projector. If a full-class display is not needed, individual students' compositions can be photocopied and handed out to the class. Whether to include the authors' names may be a judgment call by the teacher. Often it will depend on whether the students have volunteered to display their work.

When using visual displays of students' prose, some teacher direction will be needed to keep students' attention on content. Otherwise, students can be distracted by errors in spelling, grammar, or punctuation—or simply unclear handwriting. All of these things would be given greater attention if the main goal were to improve students' writing. And, indeed, in some instances there are good reasons to give attention to such matters (see Chapters 7 and 9). But the primary goal of writing for understanding is to improve content knowledge, so correcting misspellings and the like should take a back seat to discussions of substance.

In most subjects, students read information, listen to the teacher's explanations, discuss content among themselves informally as well as in formal class discussions or dialogues with the teacher, and respond to questions. In many classes, students are not given opportunities to write about the content, except perhaps to answer (usually briefly) chapter summary questions or to respond to essay test questions. When writing and class dialogues about writing are added to the class routine, the power of linguistic intersections is increased. James Britton (1987) states it eloquently:

> When talking, reading, and writing are orchestrated in the classroom in such a way that each can make its unique contribution to a single end, we have surely harnessed language to learning as powerfully as possible. Talk is then, as it were, the catalyst which ensures not only that the impact of reading upon writing shall be felt to the full, but also that there should be a feed-back effect of writing upon reading. (p. 7)

WRITING PROMPTS THAT REQUIRE CAUSE-AND-EFFECT REASONING

There is an implicit (if not, in fact, explicit) hierarchy in the writing assignments described in Chapters 2 through 6, beginning with narration, though narration is something of an "outlier," if you will, as it crosses most easily the boundary between fiction and nonfiction. Both fiction and nonfiction are valuable, because creative imagination can be a powerful means of learning even the most mundane information—perhaps *especially* mundane information. However, most writing for understanding concentrates on nonfiction, rising in complexity from relatively simple description (Chapter 3) through exposition (this chapter) and persuasion (Chapter 5) to argument (Chapter 6). Cause-and-effect reasoning similarly rises in importance as it is incorporated into these modes of writing.

Showing reasons, causes, and effects is a natural response to *why* questions. And *why* is perhaps the most often asked (or implied) type of question, particularly in high-stakes contexts, such as college entrance exams. A useful example of the SAT essay test can be found on the College Board Website (www.collegeboard.com/student/testing/sat/prep_one/essay/pracStart .html). The Website offers a sample that includes two parts. The first part is information for the writer to consider, in this case, a short passage adapted from Sara Lawrence-Lightfoot's *I've Known Rivers: Lives of Loss and Liberation:*

Many persons believe that to move up the ladder of success and achievement, they must forget the past, repress it, and relinquish it. But others have just the opposite view. They see old memories as a chance to reckon with the past and integrate past and present.

The essay assignment follows:

Do memories hinder or help people in their effort to learn from the past and succeed in the present? Plan and write an essay in which you develop your point of view on this issue. Support your position with reasoning and examples taken from your reading, studies, experience, or observations.

During the SAT, students have twenty-five minutes in which to write their essay in response to this type of prompt. Note the key phrases in the assignment: "develop your point of view" and "support . . . with reasoning and examples." This phrasing is a way of implicitly asking *why* the writer believes as he or she does.

Borda (2007) suggests another way of framing an implicit *why* question. She focuses on helping middle school students construct a thesis statement that answers the question, "What is my big idea?" (p. 30). She notes that students sometimes need practice turning a fact into a thesis and offers this example:

Fact: The blue jay is a little larger than an American robin—about 30 cm in length from the tip of its bill to the tip of its tail.

Thesis: Water pollution is a major factor contributing to the reduced number of blue jays found in the northern woodland areas of Canada (Borda, 2007, p. 30).

From the thesis, students then must respond to the *why* question implicit in it: Why is water pollution a factor in reducing the number of blue jays? That explanation forms the core of the expository composition. Borda (2007) concludes that writing expository essays "allows students to expand and deepen their ideas. Thus, all teachers have a vested interest to become teachers of writing" (p. 30).

Whether essay assignments are teacher-made or part of a high-stakes graduation exam or college entrance exam, the *why* question often is implicit rather than stated. Students need to know and practice discerning and effectively responding to implicit *why* questions.

SAMPLE EXPOSITORY WRITING QUESTIONS AND PROMPTS

Writing cause-and-effect questions or prompts that implicitly or explicitly ask *why* questions will help students master content and demonstrate such mastery. Figure 4.1 provides synonyms and near-synonyms for *cause* and *effect*—all nouns—which can be used to increase variety and specificity when composing expository writing questions and prompts.

Figure 4.1	Cause-and-Effect Terms

Cause (noun)

    Reason

    Grounds

    Source

    Root

    Origin

    Basis

    Foundation

Effect (noun)

    Result

    Consequence

    Outcome

    Upshot

    Product

Incidental "word devils" (easily confused words):

Effect (verb)—to carry out, make, or do; to bring about.
Example: A new law was written to effect a change in how certain products are taxed.

Affect (verb)—to act on, influence, or have an effect on.
Example: Some poetry has the power to affect a person's emotions.

Following are samples that teachers can use as models to develop their own assignments for expository writing that will increase students' content knowledge and understanding.

Mathematics and Science

- Consider whether you could make more money taking a job that pays $350 a week or one that pays $8.25 an hour. Think beyond the equation. What other factors might a person take into account? Then choose which job you would take and explain your reasons as you might do if you were writing for a parent.

- Define *acid* and *base*. Explain the properties of each. Then classify the following substances as either an acid or a base. Write your essay so that someone new to this class would be able to understand the following concepts quickly and easily.

Egg white

Ammonia

Stomach acid

Vinegar

Baking soda

Milk

Remind Students

- Cause and effect are not always straightforward.
- One cause may lead to multiple effects.
- One effect may have multiple causes.

Social Studies

- In the Declaration of Independence, Thomas Jefferson wrote, "We hold these truths to be self-evident, that all men are created equal." Less than a century later, President Abraham Lincoln said in his Gettysburg Address that "our fathers brought forth on this continent a new nation, conceived in liberty, and dedicated to the proposition that all men are created equal." Do you believe that these two national leaders used the phrase, "All men are created equal," in the same way? Explain your position and be prepared to read it to the class.

- Write a brief expository essay as if you were responding to a college entrance exam question, in which you identify and explain three causes of the Great Depression.

The Arts

- In a short essay, compare and contrast Vincent Van Gogh's 1888 painting, *A Café Terrace at Night*, and Edward Hopper's *Nighthawks* from 1942. Think about these night views of city cafés in terms of subject matter, historical period, and painting style. What feelings do you think each painter was trying to evoke? Why do you believe as you do? Write this essay with your classmates in mind as your audience.

- Other than the basic story, what characteristics are shared by the versions of *Romeo and Juliet* by William Shakespeare (stage play), Charles Gounod (opera), and Sergei Prokofiev (ballet)? Summarize your comparisons in two or three paragraphs. Write your essay to present this information to a classmate who is not involved in the arts.

Physical Education

- Write a brief description of English rugby football and American football, explaining the differences in the two games. If American football derived from English rugby football, why are the two games so different? Write your essay with a younger audience in mind, perhaps a student two or three grades behind you.
- Think about our class discussions of suntanning and write a short essay describing the effects of ultraviolet radiation on human skin. How do the effects of UVA differ from those of UVB? Consider your audience to be your classmates.

5

Developing Persuasive Writing Assignments

Persuasive and argumentative writing often are paired as though they were synonymous. However, persuasion and argument are different from one another and distinctive enough to merit separate chapters. Developing argumentative writing assignments is reserved for Chapter 6, while this chapter focuses on developing persuasive writing assignments. That said, the caveat with which Chapters 3 and 4 began bears reiteration— that is, no mode of writing is *pure*. There necessarily are intersections of persuasion and argument, which also intersect with description, exposition, and sometimes narration.

As writing questions and prompts begin to elicit ever more sophisticated responses, teachers and students will be increasingly interested in how well students are managing written expression. In previous chapters, the focus has been mainly on asking students to read their writing aloud. Building content knowledge and understanding is facilitated by verbal sharing followed by classroom dialogue. As students' responses become longer and more sophisticated, however, reading aloud may not be feasible. Lengthier prose is easier to comprehend—and to probe, elaborate, and expand—when students can read it for themselves, rather than only hear it.

As discussed in the previous chapter, when students begin to read their classmates' work, the urge to attend to form as well as content becomes almost irresistible. Students will incline toward pointing out and correcting distractions, such as errors in spelling, grammar, and punctuation.

Unclear handwriting may become an issue. These mechanical elements will need some attention, and Chapter 8 has been set aside to deal with common usage and punctuation questions. This chapter, like its predecessors, maintains a primary focus on content.

WHAT IS PERSUASIVE WRITING?

Persuasive writing is used to convince the reader to accept a point of view, which in most cases means persuading the reader to agree with the writer. The exception, of course, is when the writer is not writing for himself or herself but for someone else, something that speechwriters, for example, do all the time.

When persuasion is described, one often sees examples drawn from advertisements in the media, but such examples miss the point when it comes to persuasive *writing*. Auditory and visual aspects contribute significantly to the persuasiveness of ads. Similarly, the President's State of the Union address may be a *translation* of persuasive writing into oratory, but how such a speech is delivered plays a role in how well the President's ideas are received. To discern just how purely persuasive a speech or an ad is in written form, one needs to examine it stripped down to bare prose.

Persuasive writing has the following two essential elements:

1. A clear statement of opinion
2. Factual support to back that opinion

What about emotion? Can an emotional appeal be persuasive? Of course, emotion can sway opinion, but an entirely emotional appeal lacks substance and endurance. Feeling strongly about a position is insufficient support unless emotion is coupled with facts, which can be presented analytically, statistically, or through evidence, examples, or anecdotes. Support also should be specific rather than purely general.

Typically, a persuasive essay begins with an opinion statement—a thesis statement—that will direct the reader along the logical path that supports the opinion. The body of the essay presents reasoned support for the opinion. There is no set length for this section; development is determined by the nature of the topic, the audience, and other factors. The essay usually is drawn to a close by a restatement of the opinion. Also note that *essay* here is used in the broadest sense of a "piece of writing," which may be an article, a report, an editorial, or some other form.

A classic form for a persuasive essay is the five-paragraph theme, which follows this organization:

Paragraph 1 states the opinion (thesis), usually with some exposition for clarity, and announces three points that will be developed to support the thesis.

Paragraph 2 elaborates the first supporting point.

Paragraph 3 elaborates the second supporting point.

Paragraph 4 elaborates the third supporting point.

Paragraph 5 concludes the essay by summarizing these three points and restating the thesis.

There is nothing sacrosanct about this form. However, it presents a useful framework and can be condensed or expanded to suit virtually any topic.

USING PERSUASIVE WRITING

Persuasive writing requires students to use higher level thinking—that is, to process, in Bloom's terms (see Figure 1.1), at the levels of analysis, synthesis, and evaluation. Mansilla and Gardner (2008) comment:

> Today, the information revolution and the ubiquity of search engines have rendered having information much less valuable than knowing how to think with information in novel situations. To thrive in contemporary societies, young people must develop the capacity to think like experts. (p. 19)

Engaging students in persuasive writing builds content knowledge and understanding by directing students toward thinking deeply about content, forming opinions, exploring their understanding for evidence to support their opinions, and framing their ideas in thoughtful, compelling ways. This manner of thinking and writing mirrors the work of experts regardless of their field of endeavor.

To use persuasive writing as a strategic learning tool, teachers will find it beneficial to begin by dissecting an example. In a social studies context, for instance, students might be led to analyze Lincoln's Gettysburg Address (see Figure 5.1).

This speech rarely is viewed through the lens of persuasive writing, and so it offers a good example to prod students to read critically. Some background information is necessary. President Abraham Lincoln was invited to offer brief remarks—more akin to a ribbon-cutting than a formal speech—at the dedication of the Soldiers' National Cemetery in Gettysburg, Pennsylvania, on November 19, 1863. The cemetery was dedicated less than five months after the Union victory at the Battle of Gettysburg. By this point in the Civil War, deaths and injuries had risen to a quarter million, and anti-war sentiment was heightening. By the fall of 1863, Lincoln's advisors were warning him that public support for the war and for his presidency were waning.

Figure 5.1   Lincoln's Gettysburg Address

Four score and seven years ago our fathers brought forth on this continent a new nation, conceived in Liberty, and dedicated to the proposition that all men are created equal.

Now we are engaged in a great civil war, testing whether that nation, or any nation, so conceived and so dedicated, can long endure. We are met on a great battlefield of that war. We have come to dedicate a portion of that field, as a final resting place for those who here gave their lives that that nation might live. It is altogether fitting and proper that we should do this.

But, in a larger sense, we cannot dedicate—we cannot consecrate—we can not hallow—this ground. The brave men, living and dead, who struggled here, have consecrated it, far above our poor power to add or detract. The world will little note, nor long remember what we say here, but it can never forget what they did here. It is for us the living, rather, to be dedicated here to the unfinished work which they who fought here have thus far so nobly advanced. It is rather for us to be here dedicated to the great task remaining before us—that from these honored dead we take increased devotion to that cause for which they gave the last full measure of devotion—that we here highly resolve that these dead shall not have died in vain—that this nation, under God, shall have a new birth of freedom—and that government of the people, by the people, for the people, shall not perish from the earth.

In an era before modern media, Lincoln needed a way to persuade the nation, the Union, to stay the course and see the war to a victorious conclusion. The way to do so was to capture newspaper coverage, and brevity would best ensure that his words could be printed verbatim or nearly so. This calculation paid off. After Lincoln spoke, the Gettysburg Address was widely reported. Only a few people would hear and be stirred by Lincoln's delivery at Gettysburg. The majority would be persuaded by the bare prose of his remarks in print. Indeed, many newspapers carried the entire speech, which people eagerly read. Subsequently, support for the war revived, and Lincoln was reelected to a second term the following year. Today almost no one remembers or even reads the two-hour oration that preceded Lincoln's remarks, although it was delivered by Edward Everett, an acclaimed speaker and a former senator, governor, and vice-presidential candidate. Lincoln's short speech, on the other hand, remains one of the most quoted presidential speeches in history.

Does this speech follow the persuasive writing form? Absolutely! The first paragraph states Lincoln's belief in a national "proposition that all men are created equal," a viewpoint wholly at odds with the Confederacy's pro-slavery stance. Lincoln then articulates the way that this proposition is being tested by the war, the evidence literally lying at his listeners' feet in the graves of those who "gave their lives that the nation might live." While the imagery is emotional, the example is specific and factual. He then expands on the theme by stating that the living must finish the work of restoring unity to the nation by resolving "that these dead shall not have died in vain." Lincoln calls on his audience—and through newspaper coverage, the nation—to stay the course. To what end? In closing, he reiterates his thesis "that government of the people, by the people, for the people, shall not perish from the earth," thus reaffirming the national proposition of equality for all. One can only imagine how stirring this speech must have been to those fortunate enough to be present for his remarks, but most of the public read Lincoln's words and found his prose equally persuasive.

Key questions apply to persuasive writing in general—and are aptly illustrated in Lincoln's speech:

- Is the writer's opinion or position clearly stated?
- Is each supporting point factual?
- Are the points specific?
- Are the points relevant to the position?

Figure 5.2 sets these questions and related tasks into a persuasive writing template that can be used by students both to analyze persuasive writing, such as a newspaper editorial, and to plan a persuasive essay that they want to write.

Figure 5.2   Persuasive Writing Template

Topic	
Form	
Thesis (opinion)	
Supporting point	
Supporting point	
Supporting point	
Supporting point	
Supporting point	
Conclusion	

CLASS DIALOGUE

In the preceding chapters, class dialogues have been used to discuss students' writing—to validate their writing, to clear up confusion or errors, to elaborate lesson points, and to move a lesson forward. Class dialogues also can be used to model modes of writing, which may be necessary as more advanced modes, such as persuasion and argument, are introduced. In the sample dialogue that follows, the class tackles an adaptation of a writing prompt about recycling from Chapter 4. The expository writing assignment:

> Write a paragraph that you could include in a letter or an e-mail to a person living in another community. Explain our town's recycling program. Identify and give examples of at least four categories of trash that can be recycled in our community.
>
> A persuasive writing assignment about recycling might be stated as follows:
>
> City officials are considering a plan to begin paper recycling. Use your research about recycling to write a letter to the mayor or to the president of the city council to persuade this official to support the recycling of paper trash. Choose three points to elaborate that you believe will be most persuasive.

Class dialogue will help the students work through a collective persuasive writing template. The template can be projected and filled in using a computer and an LCD, DLP, or similar projector; using a transparency and an overhead projector; or using a blackboard, whiteboard, or chart paper. Otherwise students could be asked to make their own individual copy of the collective template on a preprinted form or simply in their notebooks.

See the class's completed template in Figure 5.3. Here's how the class dialogue might proceed:

Teacher: Let's work through a persuasive writing template together as we plan this persuasive letter. We'll worry about letter form after we've decided what to write. Who can suggest what our thesis should be?

Several hands go up, and the teacher calls on Nick and then Ellen.

Nick: What about "support recycling"? It's simple and direct.

Ellen: We could say something about "recycling is good for our city." That would help introduce some reasons why recycling is good.

Teacher: Let's see what others think. Remember, a thesis statement should be the writer's opinion, and the points that follow should use facts to support that opinion.

Eddie: What if we combine both ideas? We could say, "My family supports recycling because it is good for our city."

Teacher: Shall we write that in our template?

There is general agreement, and the sentence is written into the template.

Teacher: Great! Thanks to Nick, Ellen, and Eddie, we have a thesis statement. Now, what points might we use to support that statement? Let's get just the basics into our template. You'll be using the template for your individual letters later, and it will be up to you to elaborate your points.

Various students suggest points, which are written into the template.

Teacher: We have more than enough points now, and so it will be up to you to choose which points to include in your letter. What about a closing? This letter is a short persuasive essay, right? Jan, I see your hand up.

Jan: Summarize and restate the thesis!

Teacher: Exactly, Jan. Thank you. Who can give us some words to finish the template?

Once the class template has been filled in, the teacher asks students to write individual letters, which are then shared. These shared letters may be brief enough to be read aloud in a follow-up class dialogue. Or some of the students' letters can be projected, posted, or reproduced and distributed prior to a follow-up dialogue.

Figure 5.3 Persuasive Writing Template

Topic	Seeking support for paper recycling from a public official.
Form	Letter to the mayor or the president of the city council.
Thesis (opinion)	My family supports recycling because it is good for our city.
Supporting point	Recycling paper saves money.
Supporting point	Recycled paper is as good as new paper for most uses.
Supporting point	Recycling paper saves trees.
Supporting point	Our state has a company that processes used paper into recycled paper.
Supporting point	Recycling paper would save space in the landfill.
Conclusion	Summarize, restate thesis, and ask for support.

As students develop their personal letters, they use the class template as a planning tool, adding details from their research on recycling to the supporting points they want to incorporate. Following is one student's finished letter:

Dear Mayor Jamison:

My family supports recycling paper because it is good for our city. There are three reasons why we support recycling and believe you should support it, too. For one thing, it saves money. It also saves space in the landfill. And it will save trees.

If we recycle paper, then we will all save money. By recycling paper our city can save money that would have to be spent on disposing of the paper. We might even save enough money to lower taxes or be able to spend that money on other things, such as parks.

Paper that is recycled does not go into the landfill. That saves space. The landfill will not be filled as quickly and we will not need a bigger landfill. I read that every ton of paper recycled saves three cubic yards of landfill space.

Recycling paper also saves trees. This is good for the environment. Our country is not going to run out of trees, but the less we cut down the better. Trees clean the air and produce oxygen. They give shade, prevent soil erosion, and do many good things for our planet.

Saving money, saving landfill space, and saving trees are all good reasons to support paper recycling in our city. We support the recycling plan and hope you will support it, too.

Sincerely,

Jan Carpenter

PERSUASION AND THE BASICS OF LOGIC

The term *logic* often is used quite casually; *logical* is the equivalent of *reasonable*. But to be truly logical is to follow certain rules of reasoning. *Logic* has a formal meaning. It is a system of analysis that, when used correctly, helps the writer construct a persuasive letter or essay. A short study of logic can be incorporated into any subject. Its principal value is that such study encourages students to look critically at content, thus deepening content knowledge and understanding.

Logic employs a system of testing propositions, or logical statements, against one another to assess their accuracy. Aristotle, the Ancient Greek philosopher, posed this famous sequence of statements (know as a *syllogism*):

All men are mortal.

Socrates is a man.

Therefore, Socrates is mortal.

The first two statements are referred to as *premises.* If both premises are true, then logically the third statement, the *conclusion,* also must be true. However, the premises must be not only true but decisive.

In persuasive writing, this type of logical analysis can be used to test whether supporting points are logically developed. It is easy to run afoul of a logical fallacy, such as a broad generalization or a simple assertion, that, when closely examined, does not have much power to persuade.

As a follow-up to the previous assignment, students might analyze one of the supporting points from student Jan Carpenter's letter. Her second point in support of paper recycling:

Paper that is recycled does not go into the landfill. That saves space. The landfill will not be filled as quickly and we will not need a bigger landfill. I read that every ton of paper recycled saves three cubic yards of landfill space.

One way to test this point is to restate it as a syllogism:

Premise 1: Recycled paper does not go into the landfill.

Premise 2: Every ton of recycled paper saves three cubic yards of landfill space.

Which is the logical conclusion?

Therefore, the landfill will not be filled as quickly.

or

Therefore, we will not need a bigger landfill.

What might students say? If recycled paper doesn't go into the landfill and recycling saves landfill space, then it is logical to conclude that the landfill (all else being equal) will not be filled as quickly. However, some might argue that the landfill could be filled up by other material as yet undetermined; thus the conclusion that we will not need a bigger landfill is somewhat overstated.

A fair question would be, Should Jan reconsider the statement about not needing a bigger landfill? This is a good topic for a class dialogue. Both conclusions are fairly reasonable—and persuasive—given the circumstances as they are narrowly defined in this instance. The question is not whether other material might take up the space saved by not putting recyclable paper in the landfill, but whether recycling paper will make a difference by saving landfill space. All things considered, the city might need a bigger landfill in the future, but arguably it could need one sooner without paper recycling.

Most students do not learn formal logic in middle or high school unless a philosophy class is offered. But, as with cause-and-effect reasoning (discussed in the preceding chapter), knowing some of the basics of logic provides another tool for students to apply in critically listening, reading, and writing to increase and enhance content knowledge and understanding. An excellent short primer on logic basics can be found at Purdue University's online writing lab (OWL) at http://owl.english.purdue.edu/owl/resource/659/01.

OWL offers an interesting set of mathematical syllogisms to demonstrate the difference between sound logic and fallacy. The first shows how a specific conclusion can be drawn from general but decisive premises, similar to Aristotle's example about Socrates:

All squares are rectangles.

Figure 1 is a square.

Therefore, Figure 1 is also a rectangle.

In contrast, the following syllogism gets off on the wrong foot with a premise that is indecisive:

Some quadrilaterals are squares.

Figure 1 is a quadrilateral.

Therefore, Figure 1 is a square.

The conclusion, of course, is false. "Some quadrilaterals," in fact, also could refer to rectangles.

Class time devoted to basic logic and reasoning, regardless of subject matter, is time well spent. Such study will be helpful not only to improve students' writing but to sharpen critical faculties for all learning endeavors.

While we are on the topic of mathematics, it is valuable to consider whether seeking solutions to problems is always the most useful instructional strategy. This question also can apply to other subjects. Nick Fiori (2007) puts it this way:

Teachers give problems; students give answers. If only mathematics were that easy! . . . The reality is that the largest challenge in mathematics is *finding* a good problem to solve or theorem to prove—a single conjecture that is both interesting and approachable. (p. 696) (emphasis in original)

Giving students opportunities to discover problems and devise questions, to do research, and then to write will challenge them in ways that further enhance their exploration and acquisition of content knowledge and understanding.

SAMPLE PERSUASIVE WRITING QUESTIONS AND PROMPTS

Following are samples that teachers can use as models to develop their own assignments for persuasive writing that will help students explore content in greater depth and integrate new and existing knowledge to increase understanding.

> **Ask Students to Check Their Work**
>
> • Is their opinion or position clearly stated?
> • Is each supporting point factual?
> • Are the points specific?
> • Are the points relevant to the position?

Mathematics and Science

- You sell ads for the local newspaper. One 2 x 2-inch display ad costs $75 for three days or $150 for a full week. Potentially, 10,000 people will see the ad each day it appears in the newspaper. Write a short article designed to persuade an advertiser to purchase a full week of advertising. For support, consider mathematical and other practical points.
- Consider what we have studied about the properties of caffeine and the types of drinks in which caffeine is found or to which caffeine is routinely added. Write a persuasive letter to one of our U.S. senators on the position that caffeine content should be listed on drink-container labels.

Social Studies

- Thomas Jefferson is the president, and you are one of his advisors. Write a short, persuasive briefing paper on the position that the United States should go forward with the Louisiana Purchase.
- Write a persuasive guest editorial for your local newspaper that urges city government to commit public funds for a Cinco de Mayo community celebration. Use linguistic, cultural, historical, economic, or other points to support your opinion.

The Arts

- Draft a letter to your music teacher advocating that hip-hop music be taught as part of the music exploration class. What points would make your letter persuasive? Remember to rely on facts, not just opinions.

- Write a persuasive essay addressed to your classmates in which you take the position that all students should be required to learn how to draw. Consider historical precedents among your reasons that support this position.

Physical Education

- Write an editorial for your local newspaper in which you seek to persuade readers to accept the view that students should be allowed to substitute working with a personal trainer at the community YMCA/YWCA for a required physical education class at school.
- Draft a letter to the principal advocating the removal of snack vending machines from the school. Consider factors such as nutrition and economics in your reasoning.

6

*Developing
Argumentative Writing
Assignments*

Much in the argumentative writing mode mirrors persuasive writing. The caveat about intersecting modes of writing still applies. Argumentative writing also necessarily includes description, exposition, and narration at times.

By its nature, argumentative writing usually calls for lengthier prose than do less complex modes. Thus the strategies for following up on students' writing in this chapter will be similar to those discussed in Chapter 5. Students will need to be able to read one another's writing for themselves, rather than simply hear it read aloud. Of course, doing so will make it tempting for students to deal with form rather than content. That can defeat the purpose of writing for understanding. This is not to say that discussions of correct usage must be avoided at all cost. However, the primary focus must be on substance if the goal of increasing and enhancing content knowledge and understanding is to be achieved. When the time is appropriate for discussing mechanical elements, teachers will find guidance in Chapters 7 and 9.

WHAT IS ARGUMENTATIVE WRITING?

Argumentative writing is used to advance a particular position or point of view. Persuasive writing, addressed in Chapter 5, tends to be one-dimensional or single-minded—that is, focused solely on convincing the reader to agree with the writer's viewpoint. By contrast, argumentative writing is bi- or multidimensional, recognizing other positions or viewpoints and countering them to advance, by reason, a single position. *By reason* is important. As Elizabeth Martens (2007) writes, "students need to understand that *argument always involves the use of reasons and the process of reasoning*" (p. 5, italics in original).

Effective argumentative writing will require students to consider potential counterarguments. A common form is the bidimensional, or pro-and-con, argument. For example, students might be asked in the context of a class on health and nutrition or a science class to take a position on whether their school should enter into a contract with a fast-food franchise to provide cafeteria lunches in place of the district's own, more traditional food service operation. What would be the pros and cons from a nutritional standpoint? Would the higher turnover rate of most fast-food operations hold true for the school and thus ensure fresher food than the traditional school-run cafeteria? Would the often-cited negatives of fast-food (high-fat, high-salt, high-calorie content) be detrimental to students' health in the long run? Students might be asked to brainstorm lists of pros and cons and then to choose one or the other position to advocate in a written essay.

This topic could take on other dimensions if it were expanded beyond health and nutrition issues. For example, an economics class might take up the same question in a different way: Is it likely that a privatized, fast-food franchise would be more cost-effective than the school's own cafeteria operation? Would students benefit from lower lunch prices, or would they pay more for a wider menu selection from a commercial vendor? This approach also could be adapted for use in a math class to focus on numbers and ratios (prices, serving sizes, calories).

In a civics or government class, the question might be framed in terms of public versus private enterprise: Should public (nonprofit) schools contract with private (for-profit) companies to provide services, such as cafeteria lunches, that traditionally have been offered by schools through their internal operations? Should students or their parents be expected to pay the full cost of privatization, or should subsidies be available to offset the cost of commercially supplied lunches?

Once a student has adopted a point of view to be advanced, the writer then must organize an argument. The essential elements in argumentation are similar to those stated in the previous chapter on persuasion, but with the addition of a third element to address potential counterarguments:

- A clear statement of opinion,
- Factual support to back that opinion, and
- Acknowledgment of opposing opinions.

Depending on the nature of the argumentative composition, acknowledgment of opposing opinions also may include direct refutation. In other words, rather than saying, for instance, "This opposing idea is wrong (ineffective, won't work, etc.)," the writer includes reasons based on factual information: "This opposing idea is wrong because . . . ."

> **Avoid Black-and-White Thinking**
>
> Some argumentative writing can be cast in either/or terms, but on most questions, there can be a variety of positions.

Another aspect of this sample topic—directly from headlines in the popular and education press—is the long-running debate about whether to allow snack vending machines in schools and, if so, with what kinds of snacks (for example, "At high school, pit stops add 21,000 calories in two hours," *Washington Post*, May 19, 2008, accessed at washingtonpost.com).

If an argumentative essay were to be written about this aspect, a student writer might draw on press reports to make a case about whether snack vending machines should be allowed, in part by refuting the idea of changing the type of vending machines in the cafeteria. For example:

> Some people have suggested replacing one or two of our vending machines that dispense high-fat snacks like potato chips with machines selling fresh fruit and vegetables, such as apples, grapes, and carrot sticks. This strategy will not work. According to a report in the *Washington Post*, vending machine companies have tried fresh fruit and vegetable machines and the produce spoils more often than not because students prefer to buy high-fat snacks instead of healthy ones.

Note that this is only a piece of an argument. The writer might be arguing that all of the school's vending machines should sell fruits and vegetables—a "forced choice"—so that the option of high-fat vending snacks is removed. On the other hand, the writer might be arguing that students should make do with standard lunch fare and that all vending machines should be removed. Or, a third option, the writer might be arguing to keep the current high-fat snack machines because changing or removing them would prove fruitless in face of students' preference for such snacks.

This range of choices points to another common but effective instructional strategy that many debate coaches use: Ask students to consider—and be able to argue convincingly—all sides of any given issue, even those they personally oppose.

USING ARGUMENTATIVE WRITING

Argumentative writing deepens students' content knowledge and understanding by pushing students to investigate ideas and to search for information beyond classroom reading and discussion. Like persuasive writing, the articulation of a convincing argument requires students to use higher level thinking—analysis, synthesis, and evaluation, to use Bloom's terms (see Figure 1.1). All of this makes designing and using argumentative writing prompts highly productive. Such assignments also tend to be motivating, and the engaged student is the learning student.

Like other modes of writing in this book, argumentative writing is a way to ensure that students transfer content knowledge across contexts. "Unfortunately, the common methods of teaching and testing in high schools focus on acquisition at the expense of meaning and transfer," write Wiggins and McTighe (2008, p. 37). They go on to say,

> If we don't give students sufficient ongoing opportunities to puzzle over genuine problems, make meaning of their learning, and apply content in various contexts, then long-term retention and effective performance are unlikely, and high schools will have failed to achieve their purpose. (pp. 37–38)

Wiggins and McTighe (2008) illustrate what they mean by suggesting an instructional sequence that stops just short of asking students to write argumentative essays in a mathematics example using *mean, median,* and *mode.* Why not take that next step? Rather than just discussing in small and large groups the various pros and cons of each type of *average,* students might write an argumentative composition that considers all three types and argues for one as the most logical, most accurate, or fairest type to use in certain, defined circumstances.

Although Wiggins and McTighe (2008) are concerned about high school instruction, the same concerns are present in the middle school, where too often large amounts of class time are given to knowledge acquisition, while application, analysis, synthesis, and evaluation get scant attention—if, indeed, any at all. Using the mathematical concept of "average" expressed as mean, median, or mode as a vehicle for argumentative writing is fully appropriate long before high school, for example, as numerical averaging is introduced in the elementary grades.

Previous chapters have offered various approaches to using the modes of writing. In some cases, basic direct instruction is sufficient to launch students on their own, individual paths of experimental writing. This works well for narrative, descriptive, and expository writing. In other cases, such as when the student is expected to explain something quite complex or to persuade others to accept a particular point of view, instruction might more effectively proceed from an example. Chapter 5, for instance, offered Lincoln's Gettysburg Address as a sophisticated sample of persuasive writing.

Argumentative writing tends to fall into the second category, being a more complex or sophisticated mode that students may better understand initially from thorough discussion of an example. One that comes to mind that often is characterized as a form of argumentative writing is an excerpt from Chapter 9 of Mark Twain's 1883 memoir, *Life on the Mississippi,* which usually is seen anthologized as "Two Ways to See a River" (Figure 6.1). Students might be asked to read this essay and then led to dissect it in much the same way that Lincoln's Gettysburg Address was dissected in Chapter 5.

Figure 6.1   Mark Twain's "Two Ways of Seeing a River"

Now when I had mastered the language of this water and had come to know every trifling feature that bordered the great river as familiarly as I knew the letters of the alphabet, I had made a valuable acquisition. But I had lost something, too. I had lost something which could never be restored to me while I lived. All the grace, the beauty, the poetry had gone out of the majestic river! I still keep in mind a certain wonderful sunset which I witnessed when steamboating was new to me. A broad expanse of the river was turned to blood; in the middle distance the red hue brightened into gold, through which a solitary log came floating, black and conspicuous; in one place a long, slanting mark lay sparkling upon the water; in another the surface was broken by boiling, tumbling rings, that were as many-tinted as an opal; where the ruddy flush was faintest, was a smooth spot that was covered with graceful circles and radiating lines, ever so delicately traced; the shore on our left was densely wooded, and the somber shadow that fell from this forest was broken in one place by a long, ruffled trail that shone like silver; and high above the forest wall a clean-stemmed dead tree waved a single leafy bough that glowed like a flame in the unobstructed splendor that was flowing from the sun. There were graceful curves, reflected images, woody heights, soft distances; and over the whole scene, far and near, the dissolving lights drifted steadily, enriching it, every passing moment, with new marvels of coloring.

I stood like one bewitched. I drank it in, in a speechless rapture. The world was new to me, and I had never seen anything like this at home. But as I have said, a day came when I began to cease from noting the glories and the charms which the moon and the sun and the twilight wrought upon the river's face; another day came when I ceased altogether to note them. Then, if that sunset scene had been repeated, I should have looked upon it without rapture, and should have commented upon it, inwardly, in this fashion: This sun means that we are going to have wind to-morrow; that floating log means that the river is rising, small thanks to it; that slanting mark on the water refers to a bluff reef which is going to kill somebody's steamboat one of these nights, if it keeps on stretching out like that; those tumbling "boils" show a dissolving bar and a changing channel there; the lines and circles in the slick water over yonder are a warning that that troublesome place is shoaling up dangerously; that silver streak in the shadow of the forest is the "break" from a new snag, and he has located himself in the very best place he could have found to fish for steamboats; that tall dead tree, with a single living branch, is not going to last long, and then how is a body ever going to get through this blind place at night without the friendly old landmark?

No, the romance and the beauty were all gone from the river. All the value any feature of it had for me now was the amount of usefulness it could furnish toward compassing the safe piloting of a steamboat. Since those days, I have pitied doctors from my heart. What does the lovely flush in a beauty's cheek mean to a doctor but a "break" that ripples above some deadly disease? Are not all her visible charms sown thick with what are to him the signs and symbols of hidden decay? Does he ever see her beauty at all, or doesn't he simply view her professionally, and comment upon her unwholesome condition all to himself? And doesn't he sometimes wonder whether he has gained most or lost most by learning his trade?

It may be helpful to give students some background information about this (or any other) example. Samuel Langhorne Clemens, who took the pen-name Mark Twain, did so as a reflection of his early career as a riverboat pilot. Born in Florida, Missouri, Clemens and his family moved to Hannibal, Missouri, on the Mississippi River when young Samuel was four years old. Though he left Hannibal at age eighteen to try his hand as a printer, he returned to the river at twenty-two and was inspired by steamboat pilot Horace E. Bixby to take up an apprenticeship as a riverboat pilot. Clemens studied the river intensively for two years and received his pilot's license in 1859. He then worked on the Mississippi until the Civil War curtailed river travel in 1861. His first significant work, "The Celebrated Jumping Frog of Calaveras County," was subsequently published in 1865 with Clemens using his pseudonym Mark Twain, actually a river call meaning "mark of two fathoms" when sounding, or gauging, the depth of the river.

In this three-paragraph excerpt from *Life on the Mississippi*, Twain artic- ulates his thesis in the first three sentences, saying that in learning the river he had both gained and lost something of value that could never be restored to him. He begins his argument by describing an initial naïve view of the Mississippi River, using the example of "a certain wonderful sunset" full of colors and splendor—an elegant description worthy of study in itself as descriptive writing.

In the second paragraph, Twain moves to the counterargument that supports his thesis—namely, that in learning to be a riverboat pilot "a day came when [he] began to cease from noting the glories and the charms" and saw the details of the river as indicators of potential hazards: "boils," "snags," and "blind" places.

"No," declares Twain in his concluding third paragraph, "the romance and the beauty were all gone from the river." He then connects this conclu- sion to another example, that of a doctor who sees not beauty in a woman patient but looks only for symptoms of disease and decay. For Twain, knowl- edge of the river, like the doctor's knowledge of the body, forever altered his perspective. Naivety cannot be regained, in Twain's view, and that is to be lamented, as he suggests by his final question: "And doesn't he sometimes wonder whether he has gained most or lost most by learning his trade?"

There are key questions for argumentative writing—and which can be answered by this example from Twain's memoir:

- Is the writer's argument (opinion or position) clearly stated?
- Is each supporting point factual, specific, and detailed?
- Are one or more counterarguments described?
- Are both argument and counterargument(s) relevant to the position?

These questions are similar to the key questions for persuasive writing in the preceding chapter. As it was for that mode, it may be useful for students to be able to set their analysis of Twain's or some other writer's argumenta- tive composition (including their own) into a visual form. Figure 6.2 sets these questions and related tasks into an argumentative writing template

Figure 6.2	Argumentative Writing Template

Topic	
Form	
Thesis	
Argument	
Supporting point	
Supporting point	
Counter-argument	
Supporting point	
Supporting point	
Conclusion	

that can be used by students to analyze or to plan an argumentative composition. The supporting points can be increased, as can the number of counter-arguments, to suit the needs of the composition.

CLASS DIALOGUE

As was the case with persuasive writing in the previous chapter, it may be most helpful to use a class dialogue to launch students into an argumentative writing assignment. For the sake of comparison, let's take the persuasive writing assignment about recycling and rewrite it as an argumentative writing assignment. The persuasive writing assignment was stated as follows:

City officials are considering a plan to begin paper recycling. Use your research about recycling to write a letter to the mayor or to the president of the city council to persuade this official to support the recycling of paper trash. Choose three points to elaborate that you believe will be most persuasive.

A related argumentative writing assignment might be framed in the following manner:

Should the city add a paper-recycling component to its existing trash-collecting service, or should the city enter into a contract with a commercial recycling firm to collect the paper trash? What are the pros and cons of each proposition? Take a position on the question and develop an argumentative essay.

Use a class dialogue to help students work through a collective argumentative writing template by projecting and filling in the template using a computer and an LCD, DLP, or similar projector; using a transparency and an overhead projector; or using a blackboard, whiteboard, or chart paper. Alternatively students could be asked to make their own individual copy of the collective template on a preprinted form or simply in their notebooks.

The class dialogue might proceed in this fashion:

Teacher: Let's work through an argumentative writing template together as we plan this essay. Once we have the skeleton of the essay, it will be up to each of you to take a position, state a thesis—your opinion—and flesh out your own compositions. Regardless of your position, we need to know the arguments, both pro and con. Who can get us started?

Several hands go up, and the teacher calls on Steve.

Steve: The arguments are in the question, so one of them could be stated as, the city should make paper recycling part of its regular trash collection work.

Teacher: Excellent point in this case. But keep in mind for the future that not every argument will be handed to you ready-made. So, then, what about some support for this position? June, your hand is up.

June: Adding paper recycling to the current operation would allow the city to keep control of all trash collecting, and that would mean that the city also could control costs.

Teacher: Good thinking, June. Let's put that point in the template. What might be another supporting point? Caela?

Caela: The cost of collecting paper separately would be offset by money earned from recycling. The city might even make a profit.

Teacher: Shall we write that in our template?

There is general agreement, and the information is recorded in the template.

Teacher: Great! Thanks to June and Caela, we have one viewpoint sketched out. What is the counter-argument? Jason?

Jason: The city should hire a commercial recycling company to pick up paper trash to be recycled.

Teacher: Does everyone agree? *(Nods all around.)* Okay, let's write it in the template. Thank you, Jason. Now, what about a couple of supporting points.

Students suggest points that are written into the template (shown in Figure 5.3).

Teacher: Now that we have our basic arguments, it is up to each of you to decide which case you want to advocate. That means you need to fill in the "thesis" and "conclusion" boxes in the template. Then you can begin writing your argumentative essay. Try to limit your writing to three to five good paragraphs. Tomorrow we'll share some of the essays.

Figure 6.3   Argumentative Writing Template

Topic	Should paper recycling be done by the city or a contracted commercial firm?
Form	Essay
Thesis	
Argument	Paper recycling should be done by the city as part of its routine trash collection.
Supporting point	The city would control all trash collecting and so could also control costs.
Supporting point	The cost of collecting paper would be offset by money from recycling and might net a profit.
Counter-argument	The city should hire a commercial recycling company to pick up paper trash to be recycled.
Supporting point	The value of the recycled paper will pay for the company's service.
Supporting point	The city will not have to invest money in new trucks and other recycling equipment.
Conclusion	

Students develop their essays using the class template as a planning tool and adding details of their own. Following is one student's essay:

The city should begin recycling paper trash as soon as possible. Hiring another company to do the recycling might be a good idea in the short run, but it could be more expensive over time. A commercial recycling company would need to make a profit. As more people recycle their old newspapers and magazines, the company would need to expand its service. That would cost more. Also, the city is still growing. That means even more recycling and more expansion at higher costs all the time.

(Continued)

(Continued)

The city already collects our trash, and recycling paper is part of that. It's just a different way of handling the trash that gets picked up. The city must expand and upgrade how it picks up trash every few years as the city grows and older equipment needs to be replaced. So adding paper recycling as new trucks and procedures are put in place makes good financial sense. And it keeps the city in control of costs, instead of letting a commercial company charge what it wants to make a profit. The city doesn't make a profit. It provides a service.

If the city makes money from recycling paper, which seems likely, then that money can be used to help upgrade the trash trucks and treatment plants. A profit from paper recycling also could be used by the city to expand into recycling other trash, such as plastics and glass. The more recycling the city can do, the less other trash costs to pick up and get rid of. That's why I'm all in favor of the city doing our paper recycling.

FOLLOW-UP SHARING AND DISCUSSION

After developing their argumentative essays, students should be asked to share them. This can be done in several ways. In other chapters, sharing and follow-up have taken the form of a whole-class dialogue, which works well for short pieces of writing. Longer compositions, such as letters (see Chapter 5 for a persuasive letter) or essays, such as the sample in the previous section, can be displayed—posted or projected—for all students to see. Or selected essays can be photocopied and handed out so that each student has one or two to read and review. Another way to share is simply to ask students to work in small groups of three or four students and read one another's essays.

Whatever method is chosen, sharing and discussion should be shaped by a few ground rules and guidelines. The ground rules are simple:

1. *Read without preconceptions.* In other words, students should try to read as if they are coming to this subject with a minimum of prior knowledge. This is a technique that editors try to employ—to be *naïve* readers. The key is to be able to tell whether the writer is being clear and coherent without the reader "filling in the blanks" in the writer's thinking.

2. *Read from a neutral viewpoint.* Students must read as though they have not taken a stand on the issue in question, which of course will be difficult. It's easy to slide into critical mode when the writer has taken a position that opposes one's own. But for purposes of

follow-up discussion, students need to read from a neutral or undecided point of view.

3. *Use positive rather than negative criticism.* Students need to remember that the goal of follow-up sharing and discussion is to help each writer improve. This is best accomplished when the critique adopts or accepts the writer's point of view and then asks, "How can the writer's argument be strengthened?" *not*, "How can the writer's argument be countered?" *and not*, "Why is the writer's argument weak?"

Award-winning science teacher Anthony Cody (2007) comments,

When students are involved in reviewing each other's work using a clear set of guidelines, they not only have a tool that promotes honest and objective judgments, they also become more familiar with the hallmarks of quality, and they can apply that understanding to their own work as well. (p. 2)

The ground rules above are generally applicable and can be adjusted slightly to accommodate all modes of writing. Guidelines take the form of questions to guide in critiquing argumentative writing. These questions should be extrapolated from the template previously developed (see Figure 6.1). Developing these, or similar, questions is an effective group exercise in itself, as it helps students think about how to read critically not only a classmate's writing but their own.

Following are suggested questions that students should attempt to answer as they read other students' argumentative essays:

1. What is the writer's thesis? Is it clearly stated?

2. What argument does the writer pose? Is the argument reasonable or logical?

3. What points are used to support the writer's argument? Are the points factual, specific, and convincing?

4. Does the writer recognize one or more counter-arguments? What are they? How are they stated?

5. Does the writer's conclusion reiterate the thesis? Is it logical?

For a discussion of logic and persuasion that is equally applicable to argumentative writing assignments, see the previous chapter. The next chapter provides more information about how to use class dialogues to complement and extend the power of writing to increase content knowledge and understanding.

SAMPLE ARGUMENTATIVE WRITING QUESTIONS AND PROMPTS

Write questions or prompts, whenever possible, that encourage students to consider multiple viewpoints, rather than just pro and con.

Following are samples to use as models as teachers develop their own assignments for argumentative writing that will help students explore content in greater depth and integrate new and existing knowledge to increase understanding.

Mathematics and Science

- To determine which car color is most popular in their city, students stood at a busy intersection for an hour and tallied cars of various colors: red = 25, green = 5, white = 50, silver = 35, black = 40, tan = 15. How would you best show the results of their research: a circle graph, a bar graph, a tally, or a cumulative frequency chart? Write a short argumentative essay to make your case to other students in this class.
- Should basic research—research that is driven by a scientific need to know (curiosity) rather than by the need to solve a specific scientific problem—be funded publicly (by the government) or privately (through foundations and other voluntary contributions)? Compose a definition of "basic research" and consider the contributions such research makes to human knowledge. Then write a short argumentative essay to make your case for how basic research should be funded.

Social Studies

- In 1858, Abraham Lincoln and Stephen Douglas campaigned for the presidency of the United States and engaged in a series of seven debates. The main theme of the debates was slavery. Research each candidate's position. We will draw names to determine whose view you will portray in a short argumentative essay.
- U.S. Census data help shape government policies that affect how people live. Should racial categories be included in the census data that are collected? Should racial categories be expanded to include mixed, blended, or multiracial distinctions? Or should racial categories not be included in the census? Argue your position as a letter to the editor of the local newspaper that takes into account opposing views.

The Arts

- In our present age dominated by photography and graphics designed with the aid of computers, does traditional painting still matter? Consider the roles of painting in the past and how those roles are fulfilled in today's artistic world. Then write a short argumentative essay to make your case for whether painting still matters. Write as though you would put your case before a committee of teachers, parents, and students who are reviewing next year's class offerings.

- Should music that can be downloaded from the Internet be free? Consider issues concerning copyright and the rights of artists, producers, manufacturers, and listeners. Then take a position on the question and compose a brief argumentative essay to put your case before your classmates.

Physical Education

- Are sports drinks better for athletes than water? Research the issues and write an argumentative essay to make your case for a coach of your chosen sport.
- "Everyone should take a daily multivitamin." True or false? Where do you stand? Make your case in a brief argumentative essay. Think about how you might use your essay to convince your parents of your point of view.

7

Using Dialogues About Writing to Build Meaning

Ultimately writing is a solo endeavor. Whether the writer is a kinder-gartener struggling to form letters and words or a polished profes-sional who earns a living by writing, the writer must reflect, plan, compose, review, and revise one on one with a blank page or an empty screen. But before, after, and interspersed with these solo moments, students (and other writers) can benefit from content- and writing-focused discussions.

This chapter explores strategies to help students build meaning before, during, and after writing, regardless which of the modes described in the preceding five chapters they use. Each of the previous chapters explores a sample class dialogue. A *class dialogue* for the purposes of this book is a teacher-initiated, teacher-led, whole-class discussion. The class dialogue constitutes one form of discussion that will be further examined in this chapter.

The other form of discussion in this chapter is the *student dialogue*, which takes place between and among students. These dialogues may

Effective Dialogues About Writing

- Guide
- Question
- Stimulate
- Clarify
- Critique

involve students in pairs, triads, or small groups. Guidelines for such discussions usually are set by the teacher or by the teacher and students together and may be informal (such as discussed during a preliminary class dialogue) or follow a written structure, perhaps organized around a rubric. The last section of this chapter addresses developing and using writing rubrics.

A BASIS IN SOCRATIC QUESTIONING

Class and student dialogues are most effectively conducted using Socratic questioning as a basis. Named for the Greek philosopher Socrates (c. 470–399 BCE), the Socratic approach as used in education is not as formally structured as elsewhere (for example, in philosophy). The essential feature of Socratic questioning in the context of this book is for teachers to ask *authentic* questions. A feigned ignorance sometimes is helpful, but even better is a sense of "let's learn together." Authentic questions are those for which the teacher does not have answers. Often, in fact, there is no one *right* answer but many possible answers.

This general type of Socratic questioning accomplishes several useful goals before, during, and after student writing. Such questioning

- Models authentic inquiry
- Validates students' thinking
- Encourages construction of knowledge
- Increases content understanding
- Helps students solve problems

If types of questions are thought of in journalistic parlance, then the *who, what, when,* and *where* questions simply garner factual responses. It's the *how* and *why* questions that more often elicit higher level thinking and best fit the Socratic construct. This is not to say that other question stems cannot be framed for higher level thinking if attention is paid to wording. For example, asking "What reasons . . . ?" amounts to asking a *why* question. Truly open-ended questions lead to concentrated thought and debate. As Sejnost and Thiese (2007) put it: "The success of the discussion depends on the students' abilities to read analytically, listen carefully, reflect on questions asked, and ask critical, thought-provoking questions in response" (p. 125). Teachers need to model this kind of questioning in class dialogues, but they also may need to discuss Socratic questioning ideas directly so that students can successfully apply the concept independently in student dialogues.

Two useful resources on developing and using questions that elicit higher level thinking are Elder and Paul's (2006) *The Miniature Guide to the Art of Asking Essential Questions* and Chuska's (2003) *Improving*

Classroom Questions. For an excellent list of sample questions that follow Socratic questioning principles, see also Robin Fogarty's *Brain-Compatible Classrooms* (2002).

DEVELOPING AND USING CLASS DIALOGUES

Students develop writing skills, as all writers do, from practice in composing and then reviewing and revising what they have written, sometimes in comparison to other writers. Because the emphasis in this book is on developing and increasing content knowledge and understanding through writing, teachers' main focus is not on developing writing skills per se but on using writing assignments as strategic teaching tools. Full engagement in learning means that students must take active roles in learning through writing, discussion, and hands-on tasks rather than simply listening to the teacher or reading their textbooks. Beyond composing itself, such active engagement includes researching and critically reading examples of content-driven text that come from professional sources (textbooks, handouts, Websites) and the writing of their classmates *and* discussing approaches to and outcomes of writing.

Teacher-led class dialogues serve various purposes, a majority of which are dictated by when the teacher chooses to engage the class in such discussion: before, during, or after a writing assignment.

Dialogue Before Writing

Sample dialogues in Chapters 5 and 6—on persuasive and argumentative writing respectively—illustrate ways to use teacher-initiated and -led discussions to provide or supplement direct instruction about modes of writing that require students to write longer, more complex compositions.

Why not simply use a "discovery method"—that is, let students write on the basis of minimal direct instruction or discussion about the form that the writing should take? The short answer is that this type of discovery learning is a better strategy for simple concepts and simpler, more familiar modes of writing, such as narration, description, and exposition (see Chapters 2, 3, and 4). With less familiar, longer modes, students can easily become frustrated, and the process can be unnecessarily time consuming. With instructional time always at a premium, it makes good sense in these circumstances to engage students in a structured dialogue about the assignment before turning them loose to write on their own.

The idea of discovery, however, is noteworthy in a different sense. There is a reference early in this book to Langer and Applebee's (1987) seminal research report, *How Writing Shapes Thinking*, which examines the use of writing assignments "in fostering learning and integrating new information with previous knowledge and experience" (p. 3). An influential work that preceded that book, in 1970, just when the writing process movement was beginning to find its legs in curriculum development and instruction, raises a similar idea, which is expressed by its title, *Writing as a Process of Discovery.* In their book, Jenkinson and Seybold (1970) affirm the fundamental concept that the very act of writing spurs students to consider, investigate, and thus "discover" new content knowledge that the process of writing helps them connect to and integrate with their prior knowledge. This act of construction produces new understanding.

When considering how to structure class dialogues, it is important to keep this concept of writing as a vehicle for discovery and a shaper of thinking clearly in mind. Using a class dialogue as a prewriting activity usually begins with the examination of a sample composition, an exemplar of the mode that students are about to tackle on their own.

The examples in Chapters 5 and 6 are well-known: Abraham Lincoln's Gettysburg Address (Figure 5.1) and an excerpt from Mark Twain's memoir, *Life on the Mississippi* (Figure 6.1). But there is no rule that exemplars of the various modes need to be from famous writers. Indeed, quite the opposite may be true. Teachers are encouraged to build their own files of examples that are specifically related to the content they teach. Sources might include

- News, features, editorials, and columns from newspapers and online news media
- Articles from subject-specific magazines and journals, for example, *Scientific American* for science or *National Geographic* for social studies
- Excerpts from books
- Speeches (in written form) or highlights from speeches
- Online text from subject-related Websites
- Exemplars retained from previous student assignments

The last type of sample is especially useful. Once teachers have taught related content using various modes of writing as assignments, they should have a collection of examples written by students in previous classes. These examples often are more effective models than the other types because students usually relate well to the work of peers who have gone through a similar cycle of learning and writing.

In addition to introducing the structure and expectations of the writing mode, a prewriting class dialogue also should clarify specifics of the writing assignment. Jenkinson and Seybold (1970) advise:

> To respond to an assignment intelligently, a writer—student or professional—must know exactly what is expected of him. He needs to know precisely what his task is; he needs to be given help in gathering information that will enable him to complete that task if he is not a professional writer; he definitely needs to have a purpose for his writing about a specific topic; and he needs to know for whom he is writing. (pp. 10–11)

This advice can be implemented through open-ended questions that teachers might ask during a class dialogue with students before they begin writing. For example:

- Could one or two of you describe the writing task in your own words? Is the assigned mode of writing appropriate for the task? If so, why? If not, why not? (*checking for understanding*)
- How might you go about looking for information to help with the content of your writing? Might you work with other students to expand your information or share research? (*gathering information*)
- Why do you think this writing assignment might be useful for building content knowledge and understanding? What do you think the purpose of this assignment is? (*defining purpose*)
- How should audience considerations shape your writing? Who are you writing for? Who needs this information? What are the characteristics of your (real or imaginary) readers? (*identifying audience*)

Dialogue During Writing

As students are working on a writing assignment, sometimes it can be useful to take a break to allow both the teacher to assess how the assignment is going and the students to evaluate their progress. This is not the same as reviewing a first or rough draft. Any draft (even a simple outline) is a piece of writing and so falls under the next section: dialogue *after* writing.

Chuska (2003) points out that "questioning during a lesson differs from other categories of questions" (p. 36). Teacher questions to spur a class dialogue during writing would do well to follow Chuska's purposes:

- To inspire *thinking and reflection* as learning takes place
- To allow students to *review material* as learning progresses
- To involve students in *evaluating* their understanding of implicit and explicit learning
- To encourage them to "*think ahead*"—to predict, anticipate, and identify trends or patterns (pp. 36–37)

For example, a writing prompt suggested in Chapter 4 asks students studying art to do the following:

In a short essay, compare and contrast Vincent Van Gogh's 1888 painting, *A Café Terrace at Night*, and Edward Hopper's *Nighthawks* from 1942. Think about these night views of city cafés in terms of subject matter, historical period, and painting style. What feelings do you think each painter was trying to evoke? Why do you believe as you do?

Questions that a teacher could use to engage students in a class dialogue during the writing assignment might include

- Do the café settings in these paintings affect how *you* feel about the artworks? In what ways might your feelings contribute to your essay? (*thinking and reflecting*)
- What have you discovered so far about these two painters' styles of painting? (*review material*)
- As you think about what you're writing, how well are you balancing your treatments of subject matter, historical period, and painting style? (*evaluating*)
- What challenges do you anticipate having to address as you respond to the final question: Why do you believe as you do? (*think ahead*)

Dialogue After Writing

Dialogues that follow students' writing particularly ask students to be critical readers as well as writers. The composition under consideration may be a first, or rough, draft or any successive draft including the final one. The sample class dialogues in Chapters 2, 3, and 4 illustrate how the teacher can engage students in examining how—and how well—they have dealt with the content required by the writing assignment. This strategy is different from the usual follow-up dialogue that might take place in an English class, where the focus is on the writing itself. Writing assignments aimed at enhancing content knowledge and understanding should focus on content first, not that attention to conventions of writing should be entirely omitted. But certainly for preliminary drafts such attention to the writing itself is secondary, although teachers may want students to pay more attention to writing conventions when it comes to final drafts.

A content-first focus means that teachers need to lead students to discuss sample compositions by doing several of the following:

- Ensure that all students have understood the writing assignment.
- Ask students to identify how the sample writer's choice of content responds to the requirements of the assignment.
- Check with writers about their interpretations of the assignment and its requirements.
- Seek clarification and correction of content, as needed, from the writers and other students if points seem unclear or off track.
- Validate correct content and interpretation.
- Ask follow-up questions when students raise points that may need amplification.
- Introduce related content that will help students increase their knowledge and understanding and further develop their response to the assignment.

- Point out target vocabulary words or concepts with which students should be familiar and that they should incorporate into their writing.
- Draw as many students as possible into the dialogue to increase active engagement.

These discussion prompts apply whether the writing assignment calls for a simple composition or a complex one. Recall the following prompt and responses from Chapter 4 to illustrate this point:

Prompt: Yesterday we took your individual surveys of the contents of your family's trash cans and merged them into an overall description of things that people typically throw away. Based on that description how would you define *trash?* Write your definition in one or two sentences.

Response 1: Trash is stuff that people throw away.

Response 2: Trash is worthless things that people want to get rid of, such as empty soda cans, bicycle tires, plastic milk jugs, and banana peels.

The follow-up class dialogue went as follows—now with annotations (shown in italics) to match some of the above discussion prompts:

Teacher: What key characteristic do we look for in a good definition? (*ensuring understanding*)

June: I think the most important thing is for a definition to work in all cases.

Teacher: Which of these two definitions does that? (*identifying the writer's choices*)

June: The first one. It's the most general.

Teacher: But isn't it too short? Why not the second one? That sounds pretty typical to me. Brian, you have your hand up. (*seeking clarification*)

Brian: It might be typical here or even in a lot of places. But maybe people in Africa throw away different things.

Teacher: So what you're saying is that a good definition is generalizable. We're trying to define trash, not just American trash. (*validating correctness*)

Brian: Right. The second one is really more like a description than a definition.

Teacher: That's a good point, Brian. What about the idea in the second definition that trash is worthless? Is that true? (*asking follow-up questions*)

Shirley: Just because someone throws something away doesn't make it worthless. Isn't there a saying that one person's trash is another person's treasure?

Teacher: Excellent answer, Shirley. Let's talk about some of these treasures in terms of recycling. (*introducing related content*)

It is noteworthy that the teacher attempts, as much as possible, to follow a Socratic path by asking questions that are authentic—that is, questions for which the teacher does not hold the one right answer. But the teacher also is a guide, pointing students along a preset curricular path.

DEVELOPING AND USING STUDENT DIALOGUES

Sample Rules for Effective Dialogues

- Focus on content, but don't neglect the writing if there are questions or concerns.
- Read carefully before asking any questions.
- Validate the writer's effort and point out positive attributes.
- Ask questions to clarify rather than criticize.
- Make specific suggestions instead of general ones.

Class dialogues should serve as models for student dialogues. However, teachers also should set specific ground rules that students will be expected to follow when they engage in peer discussions. Often it is helpful to brainstorm these ground rules with students, but keep the rules positive, simple, and few. Posting them in the classroom can provide a ready reference.

Dialogue Before Writing

A student dialogue often can be an effective prewriting activity. Students can brainstorm, share content knowledge, and help one another organize. Peer discussions build individual understanding, and that is the goal—to enhance *each* student's content knowledge and understanding. For this reason, group writing projects are seldom as productive as individual assignments with peer and whole-class assistance before, during, or after writing.

As an example of student dialogue before writing, the teacher might give the following instructions:

We have been talking about the process of scientific discovery and how discoveries have been made in many different ways. I would like you to work in groups of three to brainstorm the names and discoveries of three scientists. For each of these three, come up with two or three keywords you could use to search the Internet for more information. Your individual assignment will be to choose one of these scientific discoveries and to write a brief expository essay in the form of a short encyclopedia entry.

Following is a sample dialogue that might take place among three students responding to this prompt:

Rick: How about Thomas Edison and the lightbulb?

Angie: That's a good one, Rick. Write it down. We could use *electricity* as one keyword.

Melissa: Didn't he try a lot of materials trying to find the best filament? What about *filament* as a keyword?

Rick: That should work, Melissa. Can we come up with one more?

Melissa: *Vacuum!* He had to create a vacuum in the lightbulb, didn't he?

Angie: Let's put *vacuum* down as a keyword, but we might get some random hits when we search, you know, like *vacuum cleaner.*

Rick: Okay, that's one. How about a second discovery?

Angie: The artificial heart.

Rick: Cool. What was that guy's name? Jarek or something, right?

Angie: Jarvik, Jarvek . . . I'm not sure if it's "i" or "e." We can check. And it was either Richard or Robert, I think.

Melissa: I've got some keywords. How about *heart, artificial,* and *mechanical?*

Rick: We'll probably need to put *heart* after both *artificial* and *mechanical* to avoid too many random hits when we search online.

Melissa: Good suggestion, Rick. Did you write them down?

Rick: I've got them. Now we need one more discovery.

Angie: How about Marie Curie and radioactivity?

Melissa: That's great, Angie! And we can use *radioactivity* as one of the keywords.

Rick: *Radium* could be another keyword.

Angie: And how about *uranium* as the third keyword?

Rick: Sounds good. That's our list then.

Figure 7.1 shows the brainstormed list created by Angie, Melissa, and Rick.

Figure 7.1 Scientific Discoveries Brainstorming Notes

Lightbulb—Thomas Edison
  Electricity
  Filament
  Vacuum

Artificial heart—Richard/Robert Jarvik/Jarvek (check spelling)
  Heart
  Artificial heart
  Mechanical heart

Radioactivity—Marie Curie
  Radioactivity
  Radium
  Uranium

Dialogue During Writing

Similar conditions apply for student dialogues as they did for classroom dialogues during writing. A useful strategy is to ask existing student groups—if peer groups were formed for dialogue before writing—to get back together to assess their progress. This is not the time to review a draft. Rather, for example, Angie, Melissa, and Rick in the previous group might discuss what they found when they went online to research their scientific discoveries. Following is a snippet of their dialogue:

Melissa: I decided to research the lightbulb. Angie, you were right about *vacuum*. That turned up lots of hits for *vacuum cleaners*.

Rick: Were you able to modify it?

Melissa: I tried *vacuum light bulb* as a keyword and really hit the jackpot with a site called The History of the Incandescent Light Bulb. That gave me pretty much everything I needed for the paper, including the fact that Edison didn't invent the lightbulb. He perfected the filament.

Rick: Wow! I didn't know that. What did you choose, Angie?

Angie: I picked the artificial heart and found out the right name: Robert Jarvik.

Rick: Did you try *Jarvek* just out of curiosity?

Angie: Actually, I did. All I got were a bunch of sites not related to hearts and a question from the search engine asking, "Did you mean Jarvik?"

Melissa and Angie clearly found success. But if, for example, Melissa had gotten stuck on *vacuum* and not come up with a modification on her own, then Rick or Angie might have suggested modifying the keyword to *vacuum light bulb* or another variation. In any case, the dialogue during writing gave these students an opportunity to check in with each other. Such peer discussions can keep individual students from getting mired in unproductive research or misdirected writing—as well as ensure that students actually are on task and making progress with the assignment.

Dialogue After Writing

The after-writing class dialogue example about defining *trash* (discussed in the preceding section) might just as effectively be discussed in peer groups of three to five students. These student dialogues might be followed by a brief class dialogue during which a spokesperson from each student group offers the group's thinking or conclusions.

This strategy of dividing the class into small student dialogue groups followed by a "report back" class discussion is useful when the topic is common to the entire class. It also works well for considering complex topics that can be broken into various components, as each student group can consider a single component. Then the *whole* can be put back together in the large-group class dialogue.

Another strategy is to ask peer groups to review the writing of their members and to give feedback within the student dialogue, rather than asking the whole class to do so. A class discussion after writing is effective for picking out exemplars, but usually there is not time to consider every student's composition. Using the peer group strategy, therefore, may be preferable as every student's work receives a critical reading by two to four of the student writer's peers.

Any of these strategies and some of the before- and during-writing strategies can be guided by general ground rules and discussion notes. Or the dialogue, whether class or student, can be guided by a formal framework, called a rubric.

MAKING AND USING RUBRICS

Rubrics isolate and thereby focus on certain aspects of a writing assignment. For many writing assignments there are dual focal points—content and form (or writing conventions). Writing assignments in the English classroom that focus on how to write, rather than what to write, tend to emphasize form. Figure 7.2 shows a basic writing conventions rubric.

Figure 7.2   Writing Conventions Rubric

Score 4—Good command of language skills

Minimal errors do not impair communication.

- Words have few or no capitalization errors.
- Sentences have few or no punctuation errors.
- Words have few or no spelling errors.
- Sentences have few or no usage errors.

Score 3—Adequate command of language skills

Occasional errors do not significantly impede communication and the writer's meaning is still clear.

- Words have occasional capitalization errors.
- Sentences have occasional punctuation errors.
- Words have occasional spelling errors.
- Sentences have occasional usage errors.

Score 2—Minimal command of language skills

Errors are frequent and some aspects of the writing may impair communication, but a reader can still understand the writer's meaning.

- Words have frequent capitalization errors.
- Sentences have frequent punctuation errors.
- Words have frequent spelling errors.
- Sentences have frequent usage errors.

Score 1—Less than minimal command of language skills

Errors are numerous and obscure the writer's meaning.

- Words have many capitalization errors.
- Sentences have many punctuation errors.
- Words have many spelling errors.
- Sentences have many usage errors.

Of course, there are much more detailed and elaborate rubrics that include categories for paragraphing and other organizational points.

A rule of thumb for using rubrics with students, whether sixth-graders or seniors, is to keep them simple and easy to understand. Rubrics are holistic in character. That is, the qualifiers in each category—"1, 2, 3, 4," or "good, adequate, minimal, less than minimal," or some other system—are applied to the composition as a whole. Individual errors are not specifically identified or quantified. The piece of writing is judged to be a "1" or a "3" based on its entirety.

Most rubrics take the form of a table or a chart. They can be structured with "scores" (as in Figure 7.2) that describe a range of characteristics, or the characteristics can be given greater individual attention. For example, "Uses complete sentences" might be rated along a three-point scale: "some of the time," "most of the time," and "all of the time." This second style of rubric tends to be most helpful as a diagnostic at the first or rough draft stage of writing because it pinpoints problem areas that the student can work on. The more comprehensive style of rubric shown in Figure 7.2 is better suited to evaluating a final draft, because it gives the student an overall sense of the success of the composition.

Teachers can take advantage of the structure that rubrics offer before, during, and after student writing. By working with students in a class dialogue before writing, teacher and students together can develop a rubric that sets expectations for the writing assignment. During writing, students can use the rubric to guide them. And then after writing, the rubric can be used either in a class dialogue or in small-group student dialogues to help students assess how well they met expectations.

For example, in Chapter 5 one of the suggested persuasive writing prompts asks science students to do the following:

Consider what we have studied about the properties of caffeine and the types of drinks in which caffeine is found or to which caffeine is routinely added. Write a persuasive essay on the position that caffeine content should be listed on drink-container labels.

Before tackling this assignment students might work with the teacher in a class dialogue to develop a rubric that highlights the major characteristics necessary for a successful persuasive essay. One type of response might be a list of key statements, such as:

- The writer's position is clear.
- The discussion of caffeine's negative properties is accurate.
- The writer's points are clear and well supported.
- The writer's argument is persuasive.

These four statements can be elaborated in a rubric that sets out levels of performance in detail, like the rubric in Figure 7.2. Or the statements can stand alone in a rubric that uses a Likert-type scale from 1 (never) to 5 (all the time) based on the class dialogue about what constitutes each response. Figure 7.3 illustrates this type of rubric.

Figure 7.3 Sample Persuasive Essay Rubric

	1 Never	2 Rarely	3 Sometimes	4 Often	5 All the time
The writer's position is clear.					
The discussion of caffeine's negative properties is accurate.					
The writer's points are clear and well supported.					
The writer's argument is persuasive.					

The references section at the end of this book includes three sources of information about making and using rubrics for various grade levels: Arter and McTighe (2000), Flynn and Flynn (2004), and Glass (2004). Of course, rubrics can be quite complex and detailed, especially when they are used in formal evaluation. (For examples, see the writing scoring rubrics from the Kentucky Department of Education at www.education.ky.gov.) But instructional rubrics should be fairly simple. Otherwise the teacher will spend more time teaching the rubric than teaching for content knowledge and understanding.

8

Internet-Writing Connections

In some circles, just mention students' use of the Internet, e-mail, blogging, or texting and let the lamentations begin: Standard English is on the slippery slope to oblivion. These doomsayers' forebears were the same ones who saw the demise of oil painting with the invention of the camera and the end of the movies with the advent of television.

"Wuts ur name?" does not spell the doom of Standard English; it offers a new language variant. Linguists label nonstandard variants in several ways: *creoles, pidgins, slang, dialects.* The French have given us the term *patois* for nonstandard language. The shorthand language of electronic communication has been called *IM-speak, e-speak,* or more generally *e-communication.* At root, it is a form of language; like Standard English, it is a code.

Most people use more than one dialect, or code, of their native language—for example, one for professional work and another when they are "down home" among family or close friends. The differences between the two may be subtle or vast. Switching from one to the other is called "code-switching." Most teachers are aware that many of their students speak to them using language that is different from the way they speak when they are among only their peers. And most students are adept at code-switching.

> **Code-Switching**
>
> Moving fluidly from one form of speech or writing to another, for example, switching from online shorthand, or e-speak, to Standard English.

When students have problems code-switching, one approach is direct instruction. Rebecca Wheeler's (2008) experiences with African-American students can point the way for code-switching in other contexts, whether the dialects of English have regional or electronic roots. Wheeler approached the challenge of code-switching by using three strategies to help her students understand and apply the conventions of Standard English when they were most appropriate:

1. *Scientific inquiry.* She led her students to examine basic language features, such as subject-verb agreement, tense, sentence structure, and sentence patterns.

2. *Compare and contrast.* She next used contrastive analysis to help students see the difference between nonstandard and standard usage.

3. *Metacognition.* Finally she taught students the idea of metacognition—knowing how one thinks—as a way to help students decide when they should use nonstandard or standard English (pp. 55–57).

The challenge for teachers has always been to help students switch codes when writing, to move from vernacular to standard usage. Now that challenge also includes helping students switch from e-speak to standard usage, to recognize that the language code of the e-mail or the text message is not the appropriate language code for writing class essays, reports, and formal letters.

USING E-SPEAK TO ENCOURAGE WRITING

Amanda Lenhart and research colleagues Arafeh, Smith, and Macgill at the Pew Internet and American Life Project begin their 2008 report, *Writing, Technology and Teens*, with these words:

> Teenagers' lives are filled with writing. All teens write for school, and 93 percent of teens say they write for their own pleasure. Most notably, the vast majority of teens have eagerly embraced written communication with their peers as they share messages on their social network pages, in emails and instant messages online, and through fast-paced thumb choreography on their cell phones. Parents believe that their children write more as teens than they did at that age. (p. i)

They then pose a significant question: "What, if anything, connects the formal writing teens do and the informal e-communication they exchange on digital screens?" (Lenhart et al., 2008, p. i). One conclusion of this study is that students themselves do not see communication over the Internet or text messaging as writing. Certainly many of their teachers would agree that e-communication hardly qualifies as writing in the traditional— Standard English—sense of the term.

Another interesting finding is that technology-savvy teenagers do not tend to write more or less than their less technologically connected peers— except for teen bloggers. Bloggers tend to be prolific writers both online and offline. Lenhart et al. (2008) found that 47 percent of teen bloggers write for personal reasons several times a week compared to only 33 percent of their peers without blogs. Furthermore, 65 percent of the teen bloggers view writing as essential to success in later life, while only 53 percent of their non-blogging peers feel the same (p. v).

Blog, for the uninitiated, is an abbreviation of *web log,* a Website maintained by an individual (or company) with regular entries, such as commentaries, descriptions of events, and so forth. The online community of blogs is termed the *blogosphere.* Blogs range from the equivalent of online diaries to independent news sources that rival commercial mass media. Another variation on the blogging idea is the online social networking site. This type of site is used to build communities of people who share interests or activities. Two of the most popular of these sites with adolescents are Facebook (www.facebook.com) and MySpace (www.myspace.com). Both of these sites allow users to "friend" others—that is, to invite friends and relatives to join their network—or to limit the number of individuals with whom they are willing to interact.

Fairfax County, Virginia, English teacher Alyssa Trzeszkowski-Giese contends, "Because we as adults haven't fully embraced this technology, we're not teaching students to use it appropriately" (Davis, 2008, p. 19). To overcome this problem, she started her own Facebook page and allowed students to become part of her network. It was an intuitive experiment, but she found positive results, such as discovering that a boy in her class who never participated—and whom she had assumed to be uninterested— actually had been paying close attention.

More and more teachers use e-mail to communicate with students and their parents, and a growing number of teachers are initiating or taking part in blogs where they interact with students. While these forms of technology present opportunities to engage students in writing and to model effective writing skills, there are some guidelines worth noting if teachers want to interact with students in the blogosphere:

- Avoid being didactic. Mentor and model rather than teach. Help students recognize the value of code-switching without denigrating e-speak; it is a valid code within its limited scope.
- "Friend" students (allow them into your blog) only if your personal information is appropriate for them in the context of a teacher-student relationship. Don't ask students to "friend" you into their personal spaces.

- Understand that Facebook and similar sites are primarily for social networking. They are not educational sites. Teachers need to maintain an appropriate social distance from students.

That being said, Trzeszkowski-Giese (2008) believes that the connection between skills being taught and interactions with students on Facebook is "a holistic approach." She comments, "You are their friend and mentor, and it gives you more credibility with them" (p. 18).

Teachers interested in exploring setting up a class blog so that their students can interact with them and their classmates might start by investigating Blogger (www.blogger.com), which is now part of Google. The Website allows users to create blogs of various kinds.

ONLINE RESOURCES CAN HELP STUDENTS AND TEACHERS

The Internet offers a treasure trove of writing-related resources for teachers and students. The Websites included in this chapter were current at the time of writing. However, Websites can be ephemeral and so it will pay to be alert for dead ends and redirections. With a few exceptions, the Websites below are hosted by nonprofit organizations, such as foundations (.org), and education entities, such as colleges and universities (.edu). But one or two worthwhile commercial (.com) sites also are included.

WEBSITES FOR STUDENTS

Online resources for students who need help with various stages of writing seem to multiply daily. Those listed below are a representative sample. A search using the phrase "student writing help" will reveal many, many more.

GUIDE TO GRAMMAR AND WRITING

grammar.ccc.commnet.edu/grammar

This site, sponsored by the Capital Community College Foundation in Hartford, Connecticut, provides a wealth of detailed information in relatively easy-to-search categories. High school students in particular will find solid, readable information to answer many questions about grammar and writing.

INTERNET PUBLIC LIBRARY'S TEEN SPACE

www.ipl.org/div/aplus

The section title, A+ Research and Writing for High School and College Students, provides step-by-step advice on researching and writing a paper, including doing research in cyberspace. A links section provides URLs for several online writing labs (OWLs).

PARADIGM ONLINE WRITING ASSISTANT

www.powa.org

This independent Website offers information in categories such as "discovering," "organizing," "editing," "documenting," and so on. Types of essays also are singled out for specific attention.

PURDUE ONLINE WRITING LAB (OWL)

owl.english.purdue.edu

Operated by Purdue University in West Lafayette, Indiana, OWL offers many resources for teachers (see Websites for Teachers) and advanced students. Sections are succinct and authoritative.

SCHOLASTIC

www2.scholastic.com/browse/home.jsp

Scholastic publishes a number of student-oriented magazines and books. The Website provides teacher resources but also has a student section with activities related to several subjects, such as language arts, math, science, and social studies.

THINKFINITY

www.thinkfinity.org

This Verizon Foundation-sponsored Website is really an online portal to free resources on other Websites. In the student section, visitors can search by keyword (such as "writing"), subject, grade level, or "content partners," meaning the actual resource providers.

UNIVERSITY OF WEST GEORGIA WRITING CENTER

westga.edu/~writing/index.htm

This is another college site, but much of the information will be useful to most high school students.

WEBSITES FOR TEACHERS

CREATING A STUDENT-STAFFED WRITING CENTER

guest.portaportal.com/wcenters

This PortaPortal.com site offers a wealth of links to resources for creating writing centers that help students and teachers across the curriculum. There are links to books, journals, individual articles, and a plethora of useful Websites.

GUIDE TO GRAMMAR AND WRITING

grammar.ccc.commnet.edu/grammar

This site, sponsored by the Capital Community College Foundation in Hartford, Connecticut, also is listed in the Website for Students section because it provides a wealth of readable information to answer students' questions about grammar and writing. It also has resources for teachers, including interactive quizzes and FAQs sections that can be adapted for classroom instruction.

NATIONAL WRITING PROJECT

www.nwp.org

The mission of the National Writing Project (NWP) is to improve student achievement by improving the teaching of writing. NWP has been around since 1974 and has nearly 200 local sites that serve all the United States and several territories. Visitors to the national Website will find many reports and resources.

PRAXIS: A WRITING CENTER JOURNAL

projects.uwc.utexas.edu/praxis

This biannual online journal is a project of the University of Texas at Austin's Undergraduate Writing Center. Like most college-level resources, this one offers much that can be adapted for middle school and high school writing projects. The journal also features a blog, which is a daily public forum for discussing writing centers. The blog welcomes writers, tutors, and teachers from around the world.

PURDUE ONLINE WRITING LAB (OWL)

owl.english.purdue.edu

Operated by Purdue University in West Lafayette, Indiana, OWL offers free online guides for writing and teaching writing, doing research, and teaching grammar and mechanics. Other resources include MLA and APA style guides, information about teaching writing in the context of English as a second language (ESL), and tips on job searching and professional writing.

READ WRITE THINK

www.readwritethink.org

Jointly sponsored by the International Reading Association and the National Council of Teachers of English, this extensive Website contains lesson plans, rubrics, teaching tips, and other information that will be helpful to all teachers regardless of the subjects they teach. The information is amplified by a large Web resource list.

THINKFINITY

www.thinkfinity.org

This Verizon Foundation-sponsored Website, also listed under Websites for Students, is really an online portal to free resources on other Websites. There are sections for educators, students, parents, and "afterschool." Teachers can search by keyword (such as "writing"), subject, grade, or content partners, including such resource providers as Read Write Think, Literacy Network, ARTSEDGE, and several others.

SCHOLASTIC

www2.scholastic.com/browse/home.jsp

Scholastic is a commercial publishing entity with numerous classroom products, many aimed at teaching writing. This Website provides lesson plans and other resources for teachers on a variety of topics.

UNIVERSITY WRITING COUNCIL @ UPEI

www.upei.ca/uwc/index.html

The University Writing Council at the University of Prince Edward Island, Canada, is a growing academic writing resource mainly intended for educators. Although the site needs much more development, it is one of the clearest to be found on writing across the curriculum (WAC). One caveat: Canadian spelling and punctuation tend to follow British conventions.

9

Frequently Asked Questions About Writing

In the context of this book, frequently asked questions (*FAQs* in computer lingo) are those questions that students (or teachers) might ask about writing. Although this book is not about developing writing proficiency per se, it seems to make sense to give teachers some answers for when students do ask those nagging questions about writing conventions.

> **Writing Conventions**
>
> *Currently accepted forms of language usage, grammar, punctuation, and spelling*

LANGUAGE ALIVE

The word *conventions* is apt. Modern languages are alive. They change, take on new words, drop older words, adopt new forms of usage, and re-invent old forms as time goes by. Today's conventional forms of word use, spelling, punctuation, and so forth may not be the conventions of tomorrow, nor were they necessarily the conventions of yesterday. Take spelling for example. Little attempt was made to standardize the spelling of English words before Dr. Samuel Johnson's famous dictionary was published in 1755. Even now, words undergo changes as they enter common usage. For example, when the bus for transporting people first came into use in the early 1800s, when it was still horse drawn, the vehicle was called an *omnibus,* from the same word in Latin meaning "for all." Through popular use, the word was shortened. In publications around the turn of the last century, it often was written as *'bus* with the apostrophe indicating the missing *omni*. Finally, the short form became the word as we know it now: *bus*. (Another form of *omnibus* survives, of course, meaning "comprising several items," as in an omnibus bill in Congress or an omnibus volume of short stories.)

A similar evolution can be seen in the word *cooperate*. When this word entered the language, it usually was spelled with a hyphen: *co-operate*. That gave way briefly to spelling it with two dots over the second *o* (called an umlaut in German, a diacritical mark rarely seen in English): *coöperate*. The mark was there to help distinguish the first long *o* from the second short *o* and to keep people from thinking the first four letters were pronounced like "chicken coop." Once the word became common enough, the aids to pronunciation were eliminated.

Most recently *e-mail* took a similar path. Electronic mail became *E-mail*, then *e-mail*, and now is most often seen without the hyphen as simply *email*.

Language changes as well as confusion about certain usage and punctuation basics give rise to the FAQs included in this chapter. What follows is by no means a comprehensive guide. There is a plethora of those on the market, and most schools (and English teachers) have several ready to hand. But these are the basics in two groups: usage and punctuation. When writing-related questions arise (and they will), these answers may prove useful.

USAGE

Some of my students write the way they do when they e-mail or text their friends, using "ur" for "your" or "you're" and other shortcuts? Should I try to correct this?

See Chapter 8 first of all. E-mail, online chat, text messaging, and the like have encouraged the development of shorthand forms of language. Some, such as *ur*, are essentially electronic pidgin. Others examples include straightforward abbreviations, such as *lol* for "laughing out loud" and *ttyl* for "talk to you later."

Language takes different forms for different purposes. When students chat with friends online or exchange e-mails, there's nothing wrong with using mutually understood shorthand. Likewise, when students are writing only for themselves, such as taking notes, the language they use online is acceptably adaptable for that purpose. Most students develop some form of shorthand for note taking or journaling. (Leonardo da Vinci wrote backwards in his private notebooks.) If the texting shorthand works for them, that's fine.

However, students also need to understand that when they write for others, they must tailor their language accordingly. This is called code-switching. Texting shorthand is not acceptable for writing a science report, for example. Teaching students about levels of formality and informality—and perhaps direct instruction in code-switching—will help them understand how best to write in various situations and for different types of readers.

I know I'm not expected to teach writing, but it drives me crazy when my students use "your" for "you're" and mix up "their," "they're," and "there." Is there any easy way to teach them to get these right?

The English language has quite a few tricky homophones, words that sound alike but have different meanings and sometimes, but not always, different spellings. For example, *rose* (flower) and *rose* (stood up) are homophones even though they are spelled the same. Teachers sometimes refer to homophones and other easily confused words as "word devils." See Figure 9.1 for a few commonly confused homophones.

Figure 9.1   A Few Commonly Confused Homophones

ad add	air heir	bare bear
been bin	boar bore	coarse course
deer dear	flour flower	gait gate
hair hare	haul hall	hear here
hole whole	its it's	knead need
know no	lose loose*	main mane
rain rein reign	sea see	sight site cite
sign sine	son sun	soar sore
stair stare	their there they're	your you're yore

Lose and *loose* are not technically homophones because they are pronounced differently, but they are commonly confused.

As is the case with learning vocabulary in general, students learn to use homophones correctly by giving them conscious attention. If class time is available, some teachers pick two or three homophones a week and simply add them to other subject-matter vocabulary lists.

What strategy can I give my students to help them learn content vocabulary?

One effective way to learn new vocabulary is for the student to use a multisensory approach that involves seeing, saying, and doing. Consider the following directions (Walling, 2006, p. 99):

Write the word.

Spell the word aloud as you write it.

Say the word.

Make up a sentence and say it aloud.

Write the sentence down and read it aloud.

Act out the word or the sentence.

For younger students in particular, this type of vocabulary building can be approached like a classroom game. If students have fun building their word knowledge, the information will be easier to learn and will stick with them longer.

In most writing for understanding, the student compositions are drafts rather than finished pieces. I know it's important for students to learn how to spell content vocabulary, but when should correct spelling in general count?

English Journal published a special issue on teaching spelling and vocabulary in March 2008, in which the best advice in answer to this question was in a "Twenty Years Ago" filler, a quote from an article by Anne Wescott (1988), who wrote in part:

Misspelled words rarely interfere with the communication of ideas, but some readers are so offended by spelling errors that they dismiss the ideas in a piece if words are spelled wrong. Teachers need to remind students that this is so and help them understand when spelling counts—in a letter applying for a job, for example—and when it doesn't—in free writing, drafts, or personal notes. (pp. 52–53)

In short, spelling correctly doesn't much matter in unshared writing or the early stages of a more formal composition. When a composition is finalized and ready to be presented to a reader, spelling counts.

I remember that active voice is supposed to be better than passive voice. How do I explain the difference to my students and get them to use active voice?

Passive and active voice are largely determined by verb use, but sentence construction (typically subject-verb-object) plays a role. Passive voice tends to be less direct and wordier than active voice, and it can be rather vague. Consider:

Passive voice: The prizes will be awarded this afternoon.

Who is going to award the prizes? Also note the long verb construction: will be awarded. The alternative is more specific and shorter:

Active voice: The president will award the prizes this afternoon.

Now we know the person who will perform the action, and the verb construction is shorter. The active voice sentence is more direct. In general, the use of active voice strengthens a person's writing. Following are a few more examples:

Passive voice: The tickets *were bought* by my mother.

Active voice: My mother *bought* the tickets.

Passive voice: My report card *seems to have been mislaid.*

Active voice: I *mislaid* my report card.

Passive voice: It *was decided* that we would each buy four shares of stock.

Active voice: We *decided* that we would each buy four shares of stock.

There are times when passive voice is the best choice, for example, if the doer of an action is unknown or the object of the action is the most important part of the sentence. In the following pair, the passive voice is the better choice:

Passive voice: The president *was rushed* to the hospital.

Active voice: Medics *rushed* the president to the hospital.

One of my students persistently misuses the pronoun I when she means me. For example, she will write "for you and I" instead of "for you and me." What's an easy way to teach her the right usage?

An easy way to teach students to check for case agreement is to separate the two pronouns in the pair and then see if the result sounds right. For example, the sentence in question is: "Let's get tickets for you and I." After the split, "Let's get tickets for you" is fine, but "Let's get tickets for

I" is not. It should be "me." So the corrected sentence is, "Let's get tickets for you and me."

The same test works for noun-pronoun pairs: "The bus picked up Sam and I." "The bus picked up I"? That doesn't work. The corrected sentence is, "The bus picked up Sam and me."

When the pronoun or noun-pronoun pair starts the sentence, the test works the same way: "Her and me went to the mall." Does "Her went to the mall" work? What about "Me went to the mall"? Neither is correct. The corrected sentence would be, "She and I went to the mall."

How can I explain parallel construction?

When multiple elements in a sentence or a list are not parallel in construction, they can make the message awkward sounding, ungrammatical, or unclear. Consider: "My errands included buying groceries, deposit at the bank, and checking my tire pressure." In this sentence, two actions are expressed by verbs ending in -*ing*. The element that doesn't fit is "deposit at the bank." *Deposit* can be a verb or a noun, and so there are two potential fixes: "making a deposit at the bank" (noun) or "depositing my check at the bank" (verb). Both fixes, however, begin with an -*ing* verb to maintain the parallel construction of the series.

The need for parallel construction also extends to lists. For example,

Our vacation itinerary includes

- A stop in a mountain village to shop
- Hiking a jungle trail
- Tour of an ancient monastery

In this case an easy fix might be to begin each element with an -*ing* verb.

Our vacation itinerary includes

- Shopping in a mountain village
- Hiking a jungle trail
- Touring an ancient monastery

Equally acceptable would be starting each sentence with a parallel noun.

Our vacation itinerary includes

- A stop in a mountain village to shop
- A hike along a jungle trail
- A tour of an ancient monastery

The best way to ensure parallel construction is to examine each element in the series and make sure that all of the elements have the same form.

What is gender-neutral language, and why is it important?

Gender-neutral language avoids stereotypical assumptions based on sex: nurses are female, pilots are male. Neither of these is true of course. Men are nurses and women are pilots. Using gender-neutral language avoids unsupported assumptions: *mail carrier* instead of *mailman, chairperson* instead of *chairman,* and *spokesperson* instead of *spokesman.* Similarly, constructions such as *male nurse* and *woman lawyer* should be avoided because the modifier (*male* or *female*) gives the appearance of exceptionality.

Often, as in some of these examples, gender-neutral language is used to replace male-dominance assumptions, such as using "operating a booth" in place of "manning a booth." *Humanity* or *human race* similarly are gender-neutral alternatives to *mankind.*

PUNCTUATION

What's a quick, easy way to explain periods, commas, colons, and semicolons?

This set of examples may be helpful:

Period (.) = Full stop, end of the sentence.

I took an umbrella with me.

Comma (,) = Pause, usually setting off a phrase or clause.

I took an umbrella, the one with blue stripes, with me. (Phrase)

I took an umbrella with me, but Maisy took a raincoat. (Clause)

Note that commas surround a phrase or clause—one before, one after—unless the phrase or clause comes at the beginning or end of the sentence.

Semicolon (;) = Stop and continue, joining two independent clauses.

I took an umbrella; Maisy took a raincoat.

Colon (:) = Introduces a list.

I took an umbrella, but Maisy took several things: a raincoat, a handbag, and a plastic rain cap.

There are many more uses of these basic marks of punctuation, but these are the most common.

What is the serial comma, and how is it used?

The serial comma (also called the Oxford comma in England) is the comma before *and* in a series of words. For example, "We ate sandwiches, chips, and pickles for lunch." Some styles, notably newspaper journalism, omit the serial comma, but that can cause confusion. Consider a book titled *Paul Bunyan, History, and Legend.* This book considers three topics: Paul Bunyan specifically and history and legend more broadly. Remove the serial comma and the title reads *Paul Bunyan, History and Legend,* a book more likely to focus on the history and legend of Paul Bunyan, one topic instead of three. Without the serial comma, "History and Legend" is an appositive of Paul Bunyan. *The Chicago Manual of Style* (2007), though it takes a minimalist approach to punctuation, still advises using the serial comma for the sake of clarity.

How do I explain apostrophes?

Most of the time apostrophes indicate possessives or contractions, but it's (note the contraction of *it is*) not uncommon for beginning writers to sprinkle in apostrophes for plurals, for example, *dog's* when they mean simply *dogs.* Lynne Truss (2003) gives a related example about teaching the difference between "Am I looking at my dinner or the dog's?" and "Am I looking at my dinner or the dogs?" (p. 26). In the former question, the dog's dinner is implied. In the latter, the person is either looking at a meal or some nearby dogs. Three main rules apply to using apostrophes:

1. Nouns take apostrophes to show possession. Examples include "John's car," "the book's index," and "my mother's cat."

2. Pronouns do not show possession using apostrophes. Examples include "its" (belonging to it) rather than "it's" (meaning it is) and "hers" (belonging to her) never "her's."

3. Contractions use the apostrophe to stand in for letters that are missing. Examples include "there's" (for *there is*, not to be confused with the possessive *theirs*), "it's" as discussed, and "can't" (for *cannot*). Of course there's also the corrupted contraction "won't" (for *will not*).

The apostrophe does mark a plural when indicating multiples of letters and numbers. For example, "Ellen got three A's and two B's on her report card." And, "Children still learn their ABC's." We also "count by 10's." On the other hand, dates used to take the apostrophe but in modern usage no longer do. For example, "FDR's presidency dominated the 1930s and

1940s." Note the possessive "FDR's" takes an apostrophe, but the era plurals that in the past would have been "1930's" and "1940's" no longer do—a reminder, again, of the changing nature of a living language.

I'm trying to get my students to use quotation marks correctly. Any tips?

Quotation marks have three main uses:

- To enclose the exact words of a quotation

  Mary said, "I think it's going to rain."

- To introduce an unfamiliar word or phrase

  In business a perquisite, or "perk," is an added benefit that comes with the job.

- To indicate that something is not what it appears

  The man said he was an expert at picking stocks "guaranteed" to double their value.

Do punctuation marks go inside or outside end quotation marks?

Periods and commas always go inside. (This is not true for British English, however.) Other punctuation marks go inside or outside depending on whether they are part of the quoted matter. For example, in the following sentence the question is part of the quote:

Jason asked, "Do you think the Cubs will win this week?"

But in this sentence the question simply includes a phrase in quotation marks:

Can anyone tell me what is meant by "revolving funds"?

10

Print Resources

To conclude this work on using writing to increase content knowledge and understanding, the following recent (published in 2000 or later) print resources are included for teachers who want to go just a bit further in the development of their students' writing skills. The titles in the books section focus on writing instruction and offer strategies for both teaching and learning. Many of these strategies can be adapted to teach content as well. A few, in fact, are content specific.

The documents section features guides and reports that are available as PDFs and can be downloaded from the Internet. The usual caveat regarding online information applies: Some Websites are ephemeral. All were current when this chapter was written, but dead sites and redirection are possible.

BOOKS

Allen, J. (2004). *Tools for teaching content literacy.* Portland, ME: Stenhouse.

> Janet Allen's book is a tabbed flipchart designed to be a ready reference for middle grade teachers to use in teaching content reading and writing. Readers will find resources on standards, assessments, and other topics, including grant writing.

Behrens, L., & Rosen, L. J. (2003). *Writing and reading across the curriculum* (8th ed.). New York: Longman.

> This 850-page volume is half textbook and half anthology. The contents are arranged in two parts. The first is a writing how-to section mainly

focused on writing summaries, critiques, and syntheses. The second part is a collection of readings arranged into subject-specific categories, including technology/communication, psychology, business, health sciences, folklore, law, and film. Readers expecting the traditional subjects of the middle or high school curriculum may find the organization confusing, but the contents are worth perusing for teachers interested in improving their own and their students' writing.

Blasingame, J., & Bushman, J. H. (2004). *Teaching writing in middle and secondary schools.* Upper Saddle River, NJ: Prentice Hall.

The authors provide strategies based on research, standards, and classroom-tested activities. Fundamental practices in the teaching of writing are examined, such as using rubrics and student writing portfolios. Also included is information about curriculum planning, service learning, and community and parental involvement.

Chuska, K. R. (2003). *Improving classroom questions* (2nd ed.) Bloomington, IN: Phi Delta Kappa Educational Foundation.

According to Kenneth Chuska, all learning begins with questions. This book helps teachers structure questions that elicit higher level thinking from students, regardless of setting. The author demonstrates how effective questions can get students to focus on concepts and principles, rather than low-level objectives.

Dean, D. (2006). *Strategic writing: The writing process and beyond in the secondary English classroom.* Urbana, IL: National Council of Teachers of English.

Deborah Dean, a former English teacher, provides hands-on strategies for helping students to think about writing as a process for inquiry and expression. Although her focus is the English classroom, the strategies will work in any setting in which students are asked to develop skills in written expression.

Fisher, D., & Frey, N. (2007). *Checking for understanding: Formative assessment techniques for your classroom.* Alexandria, VA: Association for Supervision and Curriculum Development.

Douglas Fisher and Nancy Frey's workbook-style resource book addresses the goal of giving teachers ways to strengthen their students' content knowledge and understanding with the help of creative formative assessments. The authors' suggested assessment strategies cover a broad range and include ways to use writing assignments in a variety of subject contexts.

Flynn, L.A., & Flynn, E. M. (2004). *Teaching writing with rubrics: Practical strategies and lesson plans for grades 2–8.* Thousand Oaks, CA: Corwin.

Middle school teachers will find rubrics to help them move their students' writing abilities to the next level, and the more elementary-level rubrics can be "retooled" for working with young adolescents who are struggling, have special needs, or are new English language learners (ELL).

Foster, G., & Marasco, T. L. (2007). *Exemplars: Your best resource to improve student writing.* Markham, Ontario, Canada: Pembroke.

Aimed at teachers in the upper elementary and middle school grades, Graham Foster and Toni Marasco's book presents student writing samples to accompany their description of effective strategies for teaching students how to write well. The focus tends to be mainly on essential skill development in areas such as vocabulary, organization, sentence variety, voice, and conventions.

Foster, T., & Prevallet, K. (Eds.). (2002). *Third mind: Creative writing through visual arts.* New York: Teachers & Writers.

Tonya Foster and Kristin Prevallet bring together twenty essays by teachers, writers, artists, museum educators, and others who discuss connections between writing and visual art. The title is taken from William Burroughs's phrase, "third mind," for when the confluence of two art forms creates something new. Teachers using writing for understanding in arts disciplines will find especially useful ideas in these essays.

Gallagher, K. (2006). *Teaching adolescent writers.* Portland, ME: Stenhouse.

English teacher Kelly Gallagher believes that teaching adolescents to write well should be based on six pillars of writing success, among them motivation, modeling, and a rigorous curriculum. He offers a number of classroom-tested strategies.

Glass, K. T. (2004). *Curriculum design for writing instruction: Creating standards-based lesson plans and rubrics.* Thousand Oaks, CA: Corwin.

Kathy Tuchman Glass takes readers through the curriculum design process from standards to assignments and assessments. Her model comprises four basic steps: identifying appropriate content standards, creating rubrics that set criteria for writing assessment, developing student checklists to guide students through lessons, and designing lessons to optimize student success.

Kenney, J. M., Hancewicz, E., Heuer, L., Metsisto, D., & Tuttle, C. L. (2005). *Literacy strategies for improving mathematics instruction.* Alexandria, VA: Association for Supervision and Curriculum Development.

Joan M. Kenney and her colleagues offer a content-specific resource for mathematics teachers. They include sample problems, checklists, and planning tools to show teachers how to incorporate reading, writing, speaking, and listening strategies into math instruction. English language learners and special needs students get attention in this well-rounded guide to classroom-proven strategies for students at all levels.

Kent, R. (2006). *A guide to creating student-staffed writing centers: Grades 6–12*. New York: Peter Lang.

Richard Kent, a professor at the University of Maine, believes that writing centers can help student writers work with each other and become more effective writers. His concept emphasizes student-staffed centers that support students and teachers while focusing on writing across the curriculum.

Kirby, D., Kirby, D. L., & Liner, T. (2003). *Inside out: Strategies for teaching writing* (3rd ed.) Portsmouth, NH: Heinemann.

This popular textbook had its genesis in notes about writing exchanged between a young English teacher and a young college professor. Decades later their work has been newly expanded to incorporate innovative thinking and new concepts in curriculum and instruction related to writing. This edition also includes a new resource chapter by Karen Hartman, director of the Colorado Writing Project.

National Writing Project & Nagin, C. (2006). *Because writing matters: Improving student writing in our schools*. Revised, updated edition. San Francisco: Jossey-Bass.

The authors provide ample support for their belief that "writing performance improves when a student writes often and across content areas" (p. 12), something that also affects reading comprehension. This updated edition of the bestseller includes new sections on English language learners, technology, and the writing process.

Newkirk, T., & Kent, R. (Eds.). (2007). *Teaching the neglected "R": Rethinking writing instruction in secondary classrooms*. Portsmouth, NH: Heinemann.

The title of Thomas Newkirk and Richard Kent's collection of articles echoes the 2003 National Commission on Writing in America's Schools and Colleges report, *The Neglected "R": The Need for a Writing Revolution*. Included are articles by Donald M. Murray, Tom Romano, Nancie Atwell, the editors both together and separately, and others. Topics covered in the articles range widely.

Pasquarelli, S. L. (Ed.). (2006). *Teaching writing genres across the curriculum: Strategies for middle school teachers*. Charlotte, NC: Information Age Publishing.

This volume in the Contemporary Language Education series includes articles by working middle school teachers who use genre writing to teach content and writing skills across the curriculum. Included are sample lessons, protocols, instructional materials, and assessment tools.

Popham, W. J. (2008). *Transformative assessment.* Alexandria, VA: Association for Supervision and Curriculum Development.

> Assessment expert James Popham takes a focused look at formative assessment, contending that when formative assessment is effectively done, the result is "transformative" in terms of altering perspectives on and directions of classroom instruction to better help students succeed. The author incorporates writing into some formative assessment practices.

Rothstein, A., Rothstein, E., & Lauber, G. (2007). *Writing as learning: A content-based approach* (2nd ed.). Thousand Oaks, CA: Corwin.

> The authors of this workbook-style resource present twelve strategies for engaging students in writing about subject matter. The strategies aim at building rich vocabulary and deepening students' understanding of concepts by making connections between ideas and developing organized thinking.

Ruddell, M. R. (2005). *Teaching content reading and writing* (4th ed.). Hoboken, NJ: John Wiley & Sons.

> Drawing on research and successful classroom practice, Martha Rapp Ruddell describes tested theories and proven practices for teaching reading and writing across the curriculum. Included in this volume are strategies for differentiated instruction, how-to's for using technology, and demonstration lesson plans aimed at using reading and writing to increase content knowledge.

Sejnost, R. L., & Thiese, S. (2007). *Reading and writing across content areas* (2nd ed.). Thousand Oaks, CA: Corwin.

> This resource provides step-by-step, research-based strategies that teachers can use to strengthen their students' reading comprehension and writing skills as they build vocabulary across content areas. The authors include more than forty ready-to-use masters, assessment tools, and classroom examples.

Storey, W. K. (2004). *Writing history: A guide for students* (2nd ed.). New York: Oxford University Press.

> William Kelleher Storey offers advice to students about researching and writing essays for history classes. This book covers finding topics, interpreting resources, and developing arguments. Examples are drawn from cultural, political, and social contexts. The second edition incorporates enlarged sections on plagiarism, interviewing, and Internet research.

Urquhart, V., & McIver, M. (2005). *Teaching writing in the content areas.* Alexandria, VA: Association for Supervision and Curriculum Development and McREL.

This research-based volume is designed to help teachers create time for writing, monitor what students are learning through writing, and facilitate the use of writing assignments in content classes. Published jointly by ASCD and the Mid-continent Regional Educational Laboratory (McREL), the book includes thirty-five strategies for using writing assignments to deepen students' content knowledge.

Walling, D. R. (2005). *Visual knowing: Connecting art and ideas across the curriculum.* Thousand Oaks, CA: Corwin.

Donovan R. Walling approaches the teaching of content through the visual arts. However, many of the connections between art and ideas also spark connections between writing for understanding and content across the curriculum. For example, connections between art and history naturally present topics for various forms of writing as well.

Walling, D. R. (2006). *Teaching writing to visual, auditory, and kinesthetic learners.* Thousand Oaks, CA: Corwin.

In this book, Donovan R. Walling provides an innovative resource for teachers whose picture-smart, music-smart, and body-smart learners lag behind their word-smart and number-smart peers in the mastery of writing. Included are strategies, resources, and sample lessons.

Winter, D., & Robbins, S. (Eds.). (2005). *Writing our communities: Local learning and public culture.* Urbana, IL: National Council of Teachers of English.

Editors David Winter and Sarah Robbins present a collection of tested lessons from various classroom settings, from kindergarten to college. This book comes from a multiyear curriculum project funded by the National Endowment for the Humanities and the National Writing Project that included teachers from various disciplines and institutions.

DOCUMENTS

Alliance for Excellent Education. (2007). *Making writing instruction a priority in America's middle and high schools.* Policy Brief. Washington, DC: Author. www.all4ed.org/files/WritPrior.pdf

The authors of this report state, "The role that writing now plays in the everyday experience of average Americans is unprecedented." Thus the need to make writing instruction a priority in schools is urgent. A portion of the report discusses in some depth the dual instructional goals of *writing to learn* and *learning to write* and concludes with recommendations for federal policymakers that will find resonance in local schools and classrooms.

Langer, J. (with Close, E., Angelis, J., & Preller, P.). (2000). *Guidelines for teaching middle school and high school students to read and write well: Six features of effective instruction.* Albany, NY: Center on English Learning and Achievement (CELA), State University of New York. cela.albany.edu/publication/brochure/guidelines.pdf

This report is based on a five-year study by Judith A. Langer, director of the National Research Center on English Learning and Achievement. The study compared typical education programs with those that get outstanding results, which allowed Langer and her colleagues to identify the significant features of the more effective programs.

Lenhart, A., Arafeh, S., Smith, A., & Macgill, A. (2008). *Writing, technology and teens.* Washington, DC: Pew Internet & American Life Project www.pewinternet.org

This research report was produced by the Pew Internet & American Life Project and the College Board's National Commission on Writing. The authors point out, "Teens write a lot, but they do not think of their e-mails, instant and text messages as writing. This disconnect matters because teens believe good writing is an essential skill for success and that more writing instruction at school would help them." In fact, this study found that 93 percent of teenagers write for their own pleasure—a trait that teachers might find creative ways to tap.

National Commission on Writing in America's Schools and Colleges. (2003). *The neglected "R": The need for a writing revolution.* New York: College Board. www.collegeboard.com

The authors of this report state, "Although many models of effective ways to teach writing exist, both the teaching and practice of writing are increasingly shortchanged throughout the school and college years. Writing, always time-consuming for student and teacher, is today hard-pressed in the American classroom. Of the three R's writing clearly is the most neglected." The report writers suggest a writing agenda that the nation's leaders can use to "create a writing revolution."

Salahu-Din, D., Persky, H., & Miller, J. (2008). *The nation's report card: Writing 2007.* Washington, DC: Institute for Educational Statistics, U.S. Department of Education. nces.ed.gov/nationsreportcard/writing

The 2007 National Assessment of Educational Progress (NAEP) writing assessment was administered in more than 7,640 schools between January and March 2007. Approximately 140,000 students in Grade 8 and 27,900 students in Grade 12 participated. To measure writing skills, the assessment included narrative, informative, and persuasive writing tasks. The full report includes an executive summary as well as complete details and conclusions.

References

Arter, J. A., & McTighe, J. (2000). *Scoring rubrics in the classroom: Using performance criteria for assessing and improving student performance.* Thousand Oaks, CA: Corwin.

Bloom, B. S., & Krathwohl, D. R. (1956). *Taxonomy of educational objectives: The classification of educational goals, by a committee of college and university examiners.* Handbook 1: Cognitive domain. New York: Longmans.

Borda, R. (2007, August). Teaching expository writing across the curriculum. *Middle Ground (11)*1, 30.

Britton, J. (2008). *Writing and reading in the classroom.* Technical Report No. 8. National Writing Project, August 1987. Retrieved March 17, 2008, from www.nwp.org/cs/public/download/nwp_file/151/TR08.pdf?x-r=pcfile_d

Center for Civic Education. (2009). *We the people: The citizen and the Constitution.* Level 3. Calabasas, CA: Author.

Chicago manual of style. (15th ed.). (2007). Chicago: University of Chicago. www.chicagomanualofstyle.org

Chuska, K. R. (2003). *Improving classroom questions* (2nd ed.). Bloomington, IN: Phi Delta Kappa Educational Foundation.

Cody, A. (2007, November 20). Teaching secrets: Students can do hard things. *Teacher.* Retrieved November 21, 2007, from www.teachermagazine.org/tm/articles/2007/11/20/11tln_anthonycody_web.h19.html?print=1

Davis, M. R. (2008, Spring/Summer) Classroom connections: Finding appropriate educational uses. *Digital Directions, 2,* 18–19.

Elder, L., & Paul, R. (2006). *The miniature guide to the art of asking essential questions.* Dillon Beach, CA: Foundation for Critical Thinking.

Fiori, N. (2007, May). Four practices that math classrooms could do without. *Phi Delta Kappan, 88*(9), 695–696.

Fisher, D., & Frey, N. (2007). *Checking for understanding: Formative assessment techniques for your classroom.* Alexandria, VA: Association for Supervision and Curriculum Development.

Flynn, L. A., & Flynn, E. M. (2004). *Teaching writing with rubrics: Practical strategies and lesson plans for grades 2–8.* Thousand Oaks, CA: Corwin.

Fogarty, R. (2002). *Brain-compatible classrooms.* Thousand Oaks, CA: Corwin.

Forehand, M. (2005). Bloom's taxonomy: Original and revised. In M. Orey, ed. *Emerging perspectives on learning, teaching, and technology.* Retrieved January 15, 2009, from projects.coe.uga.edu/epltt

Gardner, H. (1999). *The disciplined mind.* New York: Simon & Schuster.

Glasgow, N. A., & Farrell, T. S. C. (2007). *What successful literacy teachers do.* Thousand Oaks, CA: Corwin.

Glass, K. T. (2004). *Curriculum design for writing instruction: Creating standards-based lesson plans and rubrics*. Thousand Oaks, CA: Corwin.

Hemingway, E. (1932). *Death in the afternoon*. New York: Charles Scribner's Sons.

Jenkinson, E. B., & Seybold, D. A. (1970). *Writing as a process of discovery: Some structured theme assignments for grades five through twelve*. Indiana University English Curriculum Study Series. Bloomington: Indiana University Press.

Kendall, J. S., & Marzano, R. J. (1996). *Content knowledge: A compendium of standards and benchmarks for K–12 education*. Aurora, CO: Mid-continent Regional Educational Laboratory (McREL).

Kuhrt, B. L., & Farris, P. J. (1990). Empowering students through reading, writing, and reasoning. *Journal of Reading, 33*, 436–441.

Langer, J. A., & Applebee, A. N. (1986). Reading and writing: Toward a theory of teaching and learning. In E. Z. Rothkopf, ed. *Review of Research in Education, 13*, 171–197.

Langer, J. A., & Applebee, A. N. (1987). *How writing shapes thinking: A study of teaching and learning*. NCTE Research Report No. 22. Urbana, IL: National Council of Teachers of English.

Lenhart, A., Arafeh, S., Smith, A., & Macgill, A. (2008). *Writing, technology and teens*. Washington, DC: Pew Internet & American Life Project. Retrieved June 24, 2008, from www.pewinternet.org/pdfs/PIP_Writing_Report_FINAL3.pdf

Lester, J. (2004). *On writing for children and other people*. New York: Dial.

Mansilla, V. B., & Gardner, H. (2008, February). Disciplining the mind. *Educational Leadership, 65*(5), 14–19.

Martens, E. A. (2007). The instructional use of argument across the curriculum. *Middle School Journal, 38*(5), 4–13.

Olson, C. B., & Land, R. (2007, February). A cognitive strategies approach to reading and writing instruction for English language learners in secondary school. *Research in the Teaching of English, 41*(3), 269–303.

Popham, W. J. (2008). *Transformative assessment*. Alexandria, VA: Association for Supervision and Curriculum Development.

Rothstein, A., Rothstein, E., & Lauber, G. (2007). *Writing as learning: A content-based approach* (2nd ed.). Thousand Oaks, CA: Corwin.

Salahu-Din, D., Persky, H., & Miller, J. (2008). *The nation's report card: Writing 2007*. Washington, DC: Institute for Educational Statistics, U.S. Department of Education. nces.ed.gov/nationsreportcard/writing

Sejnost, R. L., & Thiese, S. (2007). *Reading and writing across content areas* (2nd ed.). Thousand Oaks, CA: Corwin.

SERC. (2008). *What are quantitative writing assignments?* Science Education Resource Center. Retrieved February 12, 2008, from serc.carleton.edu/sp/library/quantitative_writing/what.html

Subramaniam, K. (2008). Five tips for keeping notebooks and taking notes. *Classroom Tips*. Bloomington, IN: Phi Delta Kappa International.

Truss, L. (2003). *Eats, shoots & leaves*. New York: Gotham.

Walling, D. R. (1978). Sense exploration and descriptive writing. *Exercise Exchange*. Burlington: University of Vermont, English Department.

Walling, D. R. (2006). *Teaching writing to visual, auditory, and kinesthetic learners*. Thousand Oaks, CA: Corwin.

Welty, E. (1984). *One writer's beginnings*. Cambridge, MA: Harvard University Press.

Wescott, A. (1988). Demons, dictionaries, and spelling strategies. *English Journal, 77*(8), 52–53.

Wheeler, R. S. (2008, April). Becoming adept at code-switching. *Educational Leadership, 65*(7), 54–57.

Wiggins, G., & McTighe, J. (2008, May). Put understanding first. *Educational Leadership, 65*(8), 36–41.

Index

CORWIN

A SAGE Company

The Corwin logo—a raven striding across an open book—represents the union of courage and learning. Corwin is committed to improving education for all learners by publishing books and other professional development resources for those serving the field of PreK–12 education. By providing practical, hands-on materials, Corwin continues to carry out the promise of its motto: **"Helping Educators Do Their Work Better."**